DIALECTICS & ANALYTICAL PSYCHOLOGY

DIALECTICS & ANALYTICAL PSYCHOLOGY

The El Capitan Canyon Seminar

Wolfgang Giegerich
David L. Miller
Greg Mogenson

LONDON AND NEW YORK

First published 2005 by Spring Journal Books

Published 2020 by Routledge
2 Park Square, Milton Park, Abingdon, Oxon OX14 4RN
52 Vanderbilt Avenue, New York, NY 10017

Routledge is an imprint of the Taylor & Francis Group, an informa business

© 2020 Wolfgang Giegerich, David L. Miller and Greg Mogenson

The right of Wolfgang Giegerich, David L. Miller and Greg Mogenson to be identified as authors of this work has been asserted by their in accordance with sections 77 and 78 of the Copyright, Designs and Patents Act 1988.

All rights reserved. No part of this book may be reprinted or reproduced or utilised in any form or by any electronic, mechanical, or other means, now known or hereafter invented, including photocopying and recording, or in any information storage or retrieval system, without permission in writing from the publishers.

Trademark notice: Product or corporate names may be trademarks or registered trademarks, and are used only for identification and explanation without intent to infringe.

British Library Cataloguing-in-Publication Data
A catalogue record for this book is available from the British Library

Library of Congress Cataloging-in-Publication Data
A catalog record has been requested for this book

ISBN: 978-0-367-47800-1 (hbk)
ISBN: 978-0-367-47803-2 (pbk)
ISBN: 978-1-003-03656-2 (ebk)

Contents

Introduction
David L. Miller vii

CHAPTER 1: "Conflict/Resolution," "Opposites/Creative Union" versus Dialectics, and The Climb Up the Slippery Slope
Wolfgang Giegerich 1

CHAPTER 2: "Different Moments of Truth"—A Few Examples
Wolfgang Giegerich 25

CHAPTER 3: The Historicity of Myth
Wolfgang Giegerich 41

CHAPTER 4: Interiorizing Psychology into Itself: Following the Movement from Kant to Hegel in the Background of Giegerich's Psychology Project
Greg Mogenson 61

CHAPTER 5: Different Moments in Dialectical Movement
Greg Mogenson 77

Afterword
Wolfgang Giegerich 107

A Bibliography of the Works of Wolfgang Giegerich 113

Index 135

INTRODUCTION

David L. Miller

> "How then is it [the form of mind]
> present? ... [It is] boiling over with life ..."
> —Plotinus, *Enneads*, 6.5.12 (10).

> "Men, too, when their power of
> contemplation weakens, turn to action,
> a shadow of contemplation and reasoning."
> —Plotinus, *Enneads*, 3.8.4 (30).

A most remarkable event happened on June 3-6, 2004. A seminar was convened at El Capitan Canyon on a campground north of Santa Barbara, California. The seminar numbered a few more than two dozen members, and it featured presentations by two Jungian analysts, Wolfgang Giegerich from Germany and Greg Mogenson from Canada. This book is a record of the main presentations at that seminar, an occasion which I believe was remarkable for three reasons: the way it came into being; the fact that it may well have represented a radical advance in Jungian thought; and, the manner in which thinking was thought against the grain of a contemporary pop psychological and anti-intellectual mental health culture.

The seminar grew out of graduate course-work at Pacifica Graduate Institute during 2003 and 2004. A course in recent psychological theories of mythology was the occasion for the study of the work of Wolfgang Giegerich, a study that focused mainly on his book *The Soul's Logical Life*.[1] The graduate students wrestled with this difficult text and they found that the time available to the course did not satisfy their interests and questions. Instead of resisting or of allowing thinking to stop prematurely, they decided to explore matters further. Initiated mainly by Sharon Allen and Joshua Bertetta—but with substantial assistance from their colleagues—a proposal was made to Wolfgang Giegerich to come from Germany to California for a three and a half day seminar. With Giegerich's approval, Greg Mogenson and I were invited to be conversation partners in this event. The students had few financial resources, but they had authentic interest and openness, and, I believe, much to their surprise Giegerich, Mogenson, and I were moved to accept their invitation, not a little because of the opportunity for the three of us to be in serious intellectual conversation with each other and with interested students about psychology.

The seminar members submitted questions concerning the difficulties that they had in attempting to understand Giegerich's thinking about "the soul's *logical* life." The questions were correlated and sent off to Giegerich well in advance. He assembled the issues into three categories: misunderstandings about the nature of dialectical thinking; the problem of differentiating moments of psychological truth without leaving the domain of the psyche; and, the importance of attending to the historicity of archetypal and mythological materials. Giegerich prepared a working paper on each of these topics, utilizing examples from myth, fairy tale, and analytical practice, and he shared these papers with Mogenson and me prior to the seminar.

The seminar convened on Thursday evening and the sessions began in earnest on Friday morning. During the day, Giegerich read his prepared responses to the advance queries of the seminar members. There was

---

[1] Wolfgang Giegerich, *The Soul's Logical Life* (Frankfurt am Main: Peter Lang GmbH, 1998).

INTRODUCTION

much discussion as these presentations unfolded. On the following day, Mogenson gave a prepared response to Giegerich's reflections. There was more discussion, which lasted from Saturday into Sunday morning. Talk was intense, critical, lively, open, and challenging. People truly entertained ideas. The personal posing or taking of sides that is typical of some professional gatherings was absent. The spirit was congenial without in any way being soft. What became clear was that the work of the life of the mind—the mind of the psychologist—is difficult. The seminar exemplified and faced the truth of Jung's saying about the hard work of thinking that accompanies the soul-work of depth psychology. Jung wrote: " ... I could not confine myself to generally understandable material."[2] "It is a remarkable fact, which we come across again and again, that absolutely everybody, even the most unqualified layman, thinks he knows all about psychology as though the psyche were something that enjoyed the most universal understanding."[3] Jung even said: "As a matter of fact it was my intention to write in such a way that fools get scared and only true scholars and seekers can enjoy its reading."[4] In the El Capitan seminar the participants showed no fear. They sought as true scholars. They did not assume that they knew soul and its ways. And they worked diligently on what was not understandable in Giegerich's perspective. I don't think that I have ever, in forty years of graduate education, seen anything quite like it. There was no hint of the common contemporary *cultural* perspective on the psyche, i.e., that of New Age and pop psychology. Nor did I sense what I am afraid is a typical *academic* attitude of many graduate students: namely, that of defensiveness and resistance in the face of current academic fads or *status quo* opinions. Authentic thinking and openness (openness even to violence to one's own cherished attitudes, standpoints, and beliefs) are rare. But these were in my experience the consistent tone of the El Capitan Seminar. Ideas were at stake, not personal egos and personae. I believe that this Seminar was revolutionary.[5]

---

[2] C. G. Jung, *Memories, Dreams, Reflections*, tr. R. and C. Winston (New York: Vintage, 1965), p. 219.
[3] C. G. Jung, *Collected Works*, tr. R. F. C. Hull (Princeton: Princeton University Press, 1953), vol. 12, para. 2 (all future references to Jung's *Collected Works*, abbreviated to *CW*, will be by volume and paragraph number, designated by §).
[4] C. G. Jung, *Letters*, tr. R. F. C. Hull (Princeton: Princeton University Press, 1973), vol. I, p. 425; cf. Giegerich, *The Soul's Logical Life*, pp.13-15.
[5] I mean "revolutionary" in the sense used by Julia Kristeva in her book, *The Sense and Non-Sense of Revolt* (New York: Columbia University Press, 2000).

II

By the word "revolution," I mean to suggest that the ideas being entertained in this Seminar represented a next stage in Jungian thought. If James Hillman's work on "archetypal psychology" represents after Jung himself second wave Jungianism, the work of Wolfgang Giegerich may well indicate third wave Jungian thinking. I resist here using the terminology "post-Jungian," as some have done.[6] One does not speak of "post-Platonic" or "post-Aristotelian." Some recently have even questioned the usefulness of the term "postmodern," noting that what it designates is really another moment in "modernism." If "post-Jungian" means coming after Jung and leaving his thought, then why call it "Jungian"? If it is another moment in Jungian thinking, then why call it "post"? I prefer to think of moments of emphasis in the work of a seminal thinker such as Jung, who like other originative minds was hardly consistent and was not unchanging. "A foolish consistency is the hobgoblin of little minds," wrote Ralph Waldo Emerson in the essay on "Self Reliance."[7] Jung's mind was large and his thinking was complex. If one side is sometimes stressed, it does not mean that another side cannot be brought to articulation without a necessary contradiction of what went before.

The issue here is what it could mean to be "Jungian," since Jung himself stressed that with regard to the psyche what is crucial is to be oneself and not another.[8] James Yandell had probed this conundrum in a fine essay entitled, "The Imitation of Jung: An Exploration of the Meaning of Jungian."[9] Yandell notes that Jung had misgivings about "discipleship" as is indicated in the often-repeated saying by Jung: "Thank God I'm Jung, and not a Jungian!"[10] Even if this is an apocryphal saying, it is in the spirit of much that Jung articulated. In a letter from 1946, when Jung was 71, he wrote: "I can only hope and wish that no one becomes 'Jungian.' I stand for no doctrine ...."[11] In other letters, Jung said: "There have

---

[6] For example, Andrew Samuels, *Jung and the Post-Jungians* (New York: Routledge, 1986).

[7] See also, Gaston Bachelard, *The Philosophy of No*, tr. G. C. Waterston (New York: The Orion Press, 1968), pp. 108-114.

[8] See, David L. Miller, "Who is the True Disciple?" at: http://web.syr.edu/~dlmiller/FireMind.htm; and, Wolfgang Giegerich, "Jungian Psychology: A Baseless Enterprise. Reflections on our Identity as Jungians," *Harvest*, 33 (1987-1988): 99-103.

[9] James Yandell, *The Imitation of Jung: An Exploration of the Meaning of "Jungian"* (St. Louis: The Centerpoint Foundation, 1977).

[10] *Ibid.*, p. 5.

[11] Jung, *Letters*, vol. I, p. 405.

INTRODUCTION xi

been so many pupils of mine who have fabricated every sort of rubbish from what they took over from me."[12] "Being well-known, not to say 'famous,' means little when one realizes that those who mouth my name have fundamentally no idea of what it's all about."[13] Laurens van der Post remembers Jung as having said: "I do not want anybody to be a Jungian. … I want people above all to be themselves. As for 'isms,' they are the viruses of our day. … Should I be found one day only to have created another 'ism,' then I will have failed in all I tried to do."[14]

Yandell, therefore, speaks of the "paradox of discipleship" in the case of Jung. Yandell believes that "the only way I can emulate Jung in the deepest sense is by living out my own identity and realizing my own potential as fully as Jung lived out his."[15] This is in keeping with the notion of "discipleship" argued by Jung dramatically in the case of Christians who attempt an *imitatio Christi*, an "imitation of Christ."

> The *imitatio Christi* has this disadvantage: in the long run we worship as a divine example a man who embodied the deepest meaning of life, and then, out of sheer imitation, we forget to make real our own deepest meaning—self-realization. As a matter of fact, it is not altogether inconvenient to renounce one's own meaning. Had Jesus done so, he would probably have become a respectable carpenter and not a religious rebel to whom the same thing would naturally happen today as happened then. The imitation of Christ might well be understood in a deeper sense. It could be taken as the duty to realize one's deepest conviction with the same courage and the same self-sacrifice shown by Jesus.[16]

The "paradox," Yandell thinks, is that a "Jungian," while pursuing the path of the self's own unfolding, at the same time is one who has found the work of Jung useful in relation to her or his own. This is, to be sure, true of Jung's thinking and theorizing as well as of his life and practice. It is "Jungian" to think Jung's thinking forward, and this is just what James Hillman and Wolfgang Giegerich, each in his turn, have done, but

---

[12] *Ibid*, p. 518.
[13] Jung, *Letters*, vol. II, p. 530.
[14] Laurens van der Post, *Jung and the Story of Our Time* (New York: Pantheon, 1975), p. 4; and see Yandell, *The Imitation of Jung*, pp. 30-37.
[15] Yandell, *The Imitation of Jung*, p. 5.
[16] Jung, *Collected Works*, vol. 13 § 80-81.

not without being grounded in a radical move by Jung, which each have referred to as stressing the notion of "soul."[17]

(This paradox of influence is also the case with philosophical thought. The name of Hegel is mentioned often in the essays that follow in this book. Indeed, insights concerning the nature of a logic useful to psychology are gleaned from Hegel's thinking. But close attention to the text will show that a reader will miss the point if she or he imagines that either Giegerich or Mogenson is "Hegelian" in any wooden or dogmatic sense, a view that each is quick to contradict, as the reader will see.)

Jung had observed that in the case of the structure and function of the psyche, as Freud had said, "the ego ... is not master in its own house."[18] There are other autonomous factors in the functioning of a self. Many of these are "unconscious," a word which for Freud and Jung meant simply "not knowable,"[19] rather than being the technical term for an ego's *knowledge* of forces outside the domain and economy of ego consciousness and will. Freud referred to this revolutionary view as a "Copernican" revolution, on analogy with the displacement of the conscious human ego from the center of the universe or, in the case of Darwin, from the center of creation.[20] It is this view that distinguishes so-called "depth" psychology from humanistic and personalistic psychologies and therapies, including much that followed after Freud and Jung into the world of psychoanalytical practice and popular psychological movements, which, by comparison, represent reversions to an ego-syntonic view of self.

A key moment in seeing the radicalness of this perspective came for Jung late in his life (1958) as a result of a dream. In the dream a UFO came over the lake toward his house. He noticed that the flying saucer had a sort of "magic lantern" on it that was pointed at him. He awoke with the thought that people think that UFOs are a projection of people's ego consciousnesses, but in this dream he (Jung's "ego") is the "projection"

---

[17] James Hillman, *Re-Visioning Psychology* (New York: Harper and Row, 1975), pp. 70, 171, 189; Wolfgang Giegerich, *Soul's Logical Life*, pp. 39-43.

[18] Sigmund Freud, *Introductory Lectures on Psychoanalysis*, tr. James Strachey (The Pelican Freud Library, vol. 1; Baltimore: Penguin Books, 1973), p. 326.

[19] Jung, *Letters*, vol. I, p. 411: "The concept of the unconscious *posits nothing*; it designates only my *unknowing*." Cf. Sigmund Freud, "A Note on the Unconscious in Psychoanalysis," *On Metapsychology: The Theory of Psychoanalysis*, tr. J. Strachey, The Pelican Freud Library, vol. 11 (Baltimore: Penguin Books, 1984), pp. 45-59.

[20] Sigmund Freud, *Introductory Lectures on Psychoanalysis*, p. 326.

INTRODUCTION

of something "unidentified." In his autobiography, Jung says that this dream reminded him of another one that he had after an illness fourteen years earlier. In the earlier dream he was hiking in the mountains and had come to a wayside chapel. Inside, there was neither Virgin nor crucifix on the altar, but rather a yogi in meditation. The yogi had Jung's face. Jung awoke with the frightening thought that "he is the one meditating me." That is, Jung may well have been dreaming of a yogi from a waking (ego) perspective, but, from the perspective of the dream, the yogi was dreaming, i.e., meditating, him.[21]

Jung's thought about these dreams was that they "effect a reversal of the relationship between ego-consciousness and the unconscious, and ... represent the unconscious as the generator of the empirical personality."[22] This suggests that to view the psyche as constituted of an "ego-Self" axis, as some Jungians do, is to freeze Jung at an early phase in his thinking, an act that is itself grounded in an (unconscious) ego-perspective. From the perspective of a self (Jung's dreams and his view in later life), the soul is one and it contains the ego, among other components, in what Jung called a *complexio* and what in the El Capitan seminar was to be called a "dialectic" (see Giegerich's first presentation below).

In the early 1970s, James Hillman called for a Jungian "re-visioning," which was actually a return to the radicalness of Jung's later perspective. In the face of what he thought of as a reversion to ego's interests and perspectives in contemporary psychological thinking, Hillman stressed the need to speak of "archetypal" (an adjectival or adverbial quality), rather than "archetypes" (a noun naming some-*thing* putatively known), and of the "imaginal" and the "polytheistic" psyche (plural and perspectival).[23] His moves were intended to call attention to the "decline and fall" of the ego and its perspectives,[24] as well as to the non-humanistic ("dehumanizing") nature of a Jungian depth psychology.[25] Hillman stresses his desire for psychology's perspective in a recent work (2001) in which he was asked what was most important in the depth psychological revolution. He responded by saying:

---

[21] Jung, *Memories, Dreams, Reflections*, p. 323.
[22] *Ibid.*, p. 324.
[23] James Hillman, "Why 'Archetypal' Psychology?" *Spring 1970*, pp. 212-219; *Archetypal Psychology: A Brief Account* (Woodstock: Spring Publications, 1983), pp. 21-22.
[24] Hillman, *Re-Visioning Psychology*, p. 24.
[25] *Ibid.*, pp. 167-228.

> I follow Ernest Jones in believing that ... repression and the unconscious ... [are] the most significant conceptual ideas. To me these two ideas recapitulate Plato's 'Myth of the Cave' (*Republic*): the human being is ignorant (unconscious) and ignores this ignorance (repression). ... This view states that the unconscious is neither a region of the mind, a system of dynamic impulses, nor a reservoir of images. Rather, it is a pragmatic idea that functions to tame the Promethean urges of human *hubris*. It says: you do not know what you know; all your truths are half-truths; all your life and its actions are shadowed by unknowing. Human life is situated in a profound invisibility that can never be mastered, and you, human being, keep this ignorance out of your awareness by means of repression.[26]

Hillman's way of stressing this matter is to insist, quoting Jung, that "image is psyche",[27] which implies that all psychological knowing is imaginal in its ultimate epistemological nature.

At the Eranos Conferences in Switzerland in the 1980s (1982-1988), and especially in two later books—*Animus-Psychologie* (1994) and *The Soul's Logical Life* (1998)—Wolfgang Giegerich directed attention to a possible "monotheism" in Hillman's "polytheistic" psychology. The emphasis on "image" could have the effect of splitting *anima* from *animus*, *eros* from *logos*, synthetic from analytic, metaphorical from literal, unconscious from conscious, soul from spirit, image from word, feeling from thinking, body from mind, matter from form, underworld from daylight world, etc. In the very attempt to return to Jung's observation about the one soul being constituted as a *complexio*, a syzygy, Hillman's archetypal emphasis on image could unwittingly reinstate in its logic an ego-oriented view of psyche (i.e., the image "I" experience, the eros "I" embody, the soulfulness "I" poetize, etc.). A view of the "I" from the standpoint of the imagination is still a view of the "I".[28] Giegerich sensed the importance of thinking Jungian thought further.

---

[26] "Dreaming Outside of Ourselves," in Molino and Ware, eds., *Where Id Was: Challenging Normalization in Psychoanalysis* (Middletown: Wesleyan University Press, 2001), p. 235.
[27] Hillman, *Archetypal Psychology*, p. 14; Jung, *CW*, 13 § 75.
[28] As Giegerich has explained, the primary stress on image can unwittingly retain a subject-object split, i.e., the image or idea that I have. On the other hand, a person does not have a thought without thinking it. If a person "has" a thought, it is still merely an idea and not really achieved as a thought, i.e., as thought-ful. If one thinks a thought, subject and object, consciousness and content are one and the same. There is thought on both the subject- and the object-side.

INTRODUCTION

There was in Giegerich's argument, not a negation of what archetypal theorizing had accomplished, but rather a call to continue it radically in an attempt to complete it in its and Jung's own spirit,[29] an anima-psychology sublated[30] by an animus-psychology.[31] Giegerich says clearly: "I do not wish to claim that the soul is *not* image."[32] But, as Giegerich notes, citing Bishop Berkeley: "The soul always thinks," i.e., it also always and already is thinking, and it is therefore thought as well as image. This implies that the transformation achieved by a long-term psychological analysis will not result in real change unless the thinking that the patient brought with her or him to the analysis is also transformed.

Giegerich, like Hillman and Jung before him, is concerned to stress a non-egoic hegemony of the psyche. "The person who does psychology must be the new or *other* personality. The daimon, the Self, the soul: they are the ones who alone can produce a psychology that deserves the name."[33] But, by the same token, it makes no "sense to talk about the daimon [or self, or soul] while addressing one's thoughts *about* the daimon *to the ego personality* ...."[34] So, "the psychology *of* the Self, the soul, the daimon [can be] a huge defense mechanism against the soul, against the Self, against the daimon."[35] Giegerich writes: "This is why I said that psychological discourse has to in itself *be* a cutting edge."[36] That is, "it has to *be as* the negation of the ego, and the psychologist ... has to speak as one who has long died as ego personality. The art of psychological discourse is to speak as someone already deceased."[37] Jung had said that "only those who are relatively close to death" understand his thought.[38]

This perspective moves psychology beyond human feelings, intentions, desires, fears, and emotions. "Psychology today," Giegerich

---

[29] Giegerich, *Soul's Logical Life*, p. 104.
[30] "'Sublation' is the translation of the Hegelian term *Aufhebung* in the threefold sense of a) negating and canceling, b) rescuing and retaining, c) elevating or raising to a new level." Giegerich, *The Soul's Logical Life*, p. 67.
[31] Giegerich, *Animus-Psychologie* (Frankfurt am Main: Peter Lang GmbH, 1994).
[32] *Ibid.*, p. 106.
[33] *Ibid.*, p. 17.
[34] *Ibid.*, p. 18.
[35] *Ibid.*, p. 20.
[36] *Ibid.*, p. 24, 22. See also, David L. Miller, "The Edges of the Round Table: Eranos, Jung, and Religion," at: http://web.syr.edu/~dlmiller/Edges.htm.
[37] Giegerich, *Soul's Logical Life*, p. 24.
[38] Jung, *Letters*, vol. II, p. 536.

observes, "does not have an inkling of where the real psychological problems are. It looks in the wrong place and with the wrong categories."[39] Giegerich means to move psychology to think ego-difference differently. Already Jung and Hillman had a sense of this need. Jung had already written: "The thoughts of the patient must be taken seriously."[40] "They [the patients] adapt only as far as they can grasp the situation intellectually."[41] This perspective of Jung's is often ignored by contemporary Jungians in both theory and practice. But it was a theme of Hillman's writing, as well as of Jung's. Hillman had written in his Terry Lectures at Yale: "A psyche with few psychological ideas is easily a victim. ... The discussion of ideas in therapy is not necessarily a defense against emotion but the preliminary to emotion and the carrier of it."[42] Hillman had insisted that ideas, as well as soul, and for the sake of soul, need therapy.[43]

But Giegerich prosecuted this perspective in a new way. "It is not sufficient," he said in *Spring* journal in 1987, "to propound the 'right' ideas. ... For these 'right' ideas are placed into a world whose logic remains unchanged. Even worse, into these 'right' ideas themselves is invested the old logic, and they unwittingly perpetuate the very thing that they mean to heal."[44] "Even while *talking* a lot about transformation and change [as both Jung and Hillman had done before], indeed about initiation, death and the underworld, psychology itself, in how it speaks and writes about these and all other themes, supports the unbroken continuity of the old ego"[45] and its logic. The implication is that the life of psychological transformation depends in part on the transformation of soul's logic. Thinking is *psychologically* crucial.[46] As Giegerich puts it:

---

[39] Giegerich, *Soul's Logical Life*, p. 31.
[40] Jung, *Collected Works*, vol. 3 § 421.
[41] *Ibid.*, § 417.
[42] Hillman, *Re-Visioning Psychology*, pp. 118, 120.
[43] Hillman and Ventura, *We've Had a Hundred Years of Psychotherapy—and the World is Getting Worse* (San Francisco: HarperSanFrancisco, 1992), pp. 16, 25, 66-68, 82, 107, 141-145, 171, 191; see also, David L. Miller, "Animadversions," *Spring*, pp. 26-29. But see the comment in footnote 28, above.
[44] Wolfgang Giegerich, "The Rescue of the World: Jung, Hegel, and the Subjective Universe," *Spring*, 1987: 113-114; cf. Giegerich, *Soul's Logical Life*, p. 18.
[45] Giegerich, *Soul's Logical Life*, p. 16.
[46] See: Debra Knowles, *Along a Path Apart: Conflict and Concordance in C. G. Jung and Martin Heidegger* (Ann Arbor: ProQuest, 2002); and, Toshio Kawai, *Bild und Sprache und ihre Beziehung zur Welt: Überlegungen zur Bedeutung von Jung und Heidegger für die Psychologie* (Würzburg: Königshausen & Neumann, 1988).

INTRODUCTION   xvii

"Abstract thinking is what today's *soul* needs. It is the soul that requires more intellect. The soul does not need more feelings, emotions, body work. All this is [still] ego-stuff."[47] This, in my view, marks a radical move in Jungian thinking, third-wave Jungianism, even though it is a move incipiently present in the work of Jung and Hillman.

III

What the El Capitan seminar demonstrated, however, is that it is not a simple matter to think *psychologically* about "intellect" and "thinking." My own experience, not only of the seminar in California, but also in forty years of graduate education, is that there seems to be, not only an American anti-intellectualism reigning in the contemporary cultural consciousness,[48] and, to be sure, not only in the United States, but also a perspective that thinks that thinking is moving counters (ideas) around willfully in the brain, a sort of mock-Cartesian rationalism and one-sided intellectualism. This is clearly not what Giegerich is talking about and it is one of the stumbling blocks that I have encountered in the attempt to teach Giegerich's work. Thinking needs to be thought, and, indeed, a third remarkable quality of the El Capitan seminar was its attempt to think thinking differently, i.e., psychologically. The clue for this attempt was an understanding of the nature of dialectical thinking (concerning which there was some initial misunderstanding on the part of the seminar participants) and the importance of the negative (concerning which there was a bit of resistance).

I first sensed this difficulty in understanding Giegerich's thinking about thinking and logic during an online seminar sponsored by the C. G. Jung website (www.cgjungpage.org) in October of 1998. On the final day of that cyberseminar, I posted a question to Giegerich, saying that I thought that his interlocutors were misunderstanding his notion of thinking, and that they were critiquing a position that they were projecting onto him, a position that he did not hold. That is, they were demonizing thinking, taking it to be the opposite of feeling (*logos* over against *eros*), and then wondering why he was privileging it in psychological work. I asked him to clarify

---
[47] Giegerich, *Soul's Logical Life*, p. 31.
[48] See: Richard Hofstadter, *Anti-intellectualism in American Life* (New York: Knopf, 1963).

what he meant by the soul's *logical* life in which thinking is crucial to psychological transformation.

My query came late in the seminar, just before its close, and Giegerich's response was necessarily shortened by the constraints of the online discussion. In a private[49] e-mail correspondence on the following day, I tried to clarify what I saw as the misunderstanding by the seminar participants. Giegerich had mentioned a work by Martin Heidegger, *Aus der Erfahrung des Denkens* ("Out of the Experience of Thinking") in his book, *The Soul's Logical Life*,[50] just as he also invokes the language of Heidegger (*die Schritt zurück*) in the current volume when making a point about the nature of the Hegelian dialectic. In my note to Giegerich, I reminded him of a distinction Heidegger makes in another book, *Gelassenheit* ("Discourse on Thinking"), between *das rechnende Denken* and *das besinnliche Nachdenken*, which the English translator of this work renders "calculative thinking" and "meditative thinking."[51] The translations do not really carry the force of Heidegger's language. "Calculative" is not inappropriate for *rechnende*, since *rechnen* means "to calculate, compute, count, or reckon" and *der Rechner* is the current German term for a "calculator" or "computer." But "meditative" overdetermines *besinnlich* in the direction of Romantic or spiritual sensibility. The German adjective normally means "contemplative" or "thought provoking," and nowhere in the English translation is there an indication that in one case *Denken* is used and in the other case the term is *Nachdenken*. This latter word means more than thinking. It indicates cogitating or mulling *over* or thinking *about* or musing or *re*flecting, i.e., it indicates a process and an activity. My hunch was that Giegerich's conversation partners in the cyberseminar thought that he meant *das rechnende Denken*—what my grandmother in Virginia used to mean when she said, "Well, I reckon ...." It had seemed to me that when Giegerich spoke about "thinking" or "logic," what he actually had in mind was more like Heidegger's *das besinnliche Nachdenken*. Giegerich wrote back to me that I was right about this and he indicated that with this misunderstanding he could

---

[49] I have Wolfgang Giegerich's permission to share this anecdote.
[50] Giegerich, *Soul's Logical Life*, p. 43.
[51] Martin Heidegger, *Gelassenheit* (Pfullingen: Neske, 1959), pp. 15-16; *Discourse on Thinking*, tr. J. Anderson and E. H. Freund (New York: Harper, 1966), pp. 46-47.

INTRODUCTION

see why his questioners were critical about his psychological stress on "thinking."

However, Giegerich had second thoughts (a *Nach-denken* or "after-thought") two years later. On February 23rd, 2000, he wrote to me the following:

> ... this distinction of Heidegger's is a bit problematic for me. He (a) splits, setting up a special, privileged kind of thinking (sort of a Sunday-version of it) where in my opinion there should not be a diastema, and (b) he uses this distinction to (unfairly) condemn classical metaphysics, which he places on the side of *das rechnende Denken*, a retrojection of our modern problem into the past. For me thought is one, and if it is pushed forward far enough beyond the initial pragmatic ... version of it, it becomes dialectical...."[52]

The point is, in part, that reckoning, counting, computing, and calculating are important parts of thinking. One might think of such as the instrumental aspect of thinking, but, of course, to think that this is all that thinking is is itself thoughtless.

I mention this older exchange in order to introduce the discussion of "dialectics" which follows in this book, i.e., in order to show that psychological thinking about thinking is not simple. For example, thinking—in the sense that it will be talked about in the El Capitan seminar—is not a psychological function.[53] That is, it is not one of Jung's ectopsychic functions alongside feeling, sensation and intuition, and it is, therefore, not something done, or done well, only by so-called "thinking types." Rather, everyone, regardless of typology, is a thinker in the sense that Aristotle may have meant by calling the human being an *animal rationale*. To be sure, thinking is unconscious in most persons most of the time. It is implicit thinking. But it is not not-thinking. Thinking also is not to be thought of as mere abstract and formal logic, nor is it merely discursive reasoning or the literal employment of the intellect. Rather, it is concrete, a real movement of the soul.[54] Thinking

---

[52] E-mail from Wolfgang Giegerich to David Miller, February 23, 2000, used here with the knowledge and permission of the author.

[53] Giegerich, *Soul's Logical Life*, p. 44; *Der jungsche Begriff der Neurose* (Frankfurt am Main: Peter Lang GmbH, 1999), pp. 20-21.

[54] Wolfgang Giegerich, "The Opposition of 'Individual' and 'Collective' Psychology's Basic Fault: Reflections On Today's Magnum Opus of the Soul," *Harvest*, 42.2 (1996): 7-27; *Soul's Logical Life*, p. 113.

means having been reached or claimed by a thought. Heidegger, in the work that Giegerich cites in *The Soul's Logical Life*, says: "We never come to thoughts. They come to us."[55]

The problem then is unconscious thought and what Heidegger calls *die Flucht vor dem Denken*, the "flight from thought." Psychology today, too, has been thoughtless and has been a participant in this "flight." Psychologically this flight indicates an unconscious fear (what Freud called *Gedankenschreck*, "fear of thinking"[56]), even for psychology itself. It is, to be sure, a defense precisely against what in this book will be called dialectics in which one may discover (make conscious) not only a logic and a thought, but, also and at the same time, the reality of that thought's negation, not as a positive thing, but as a positive-negative, which also will in the process of thinking or in the course of time need to be negated (the negation of the negation). Psychologically, this process of dialectical thinking can transform ego's fixations by showing them to be moments within the self, which is one and outside of which there is no-thing.[57] This is radical psychology and it implies that thinking about thinking can result in psychological, i.e., soulful, life.

There is ancient precedence for this perspective. For example, it is represented in the epigraphs that begin this Introduction. In the third century B.C.E., Plotinus taught his students that mind (*nous*) is, as he put it, "boiling over with life."[58] Thinking makes life lively. Plotinus may have gotten this from Aristotle.[59] Aristotle says that pre-Socratic ideas about soul and life followed their etymologies and so people thought of "soul" as "hot." This notion makes sense only when one realizes that the Greek text of Plotinus carries a pun. Plotinus's Greek text reads: *hyperzeousan zōē*, "boiling with life." *Zēn*, "live," and *zein*, "boil," are homophones. Life is hot! Plotinus is not talking about ego's life or ego's sensibility, but the life and soul of self. To live in a self is to

---

[55] Martin Heidegger, *Aus der Erfahrung des Denkens* (Pfullingen: Neske, 1965), p. 11: "Wir kommen nie zu Gedanken. Sie kommen zu uns."

[56] Freud uses this term when reporting one of his own dreams. The dream produced considerable anxiety and he reports that he awoke in what the standard translation renders with the phrase "mental fright," i.e., a fear of thinking about (*Gedankenschreck*) the dream and its logic. See: Sigmund Freud, *Interpretation of Dreams*, tr. James Strachey, The Pelican Freud Library (Baltimore: Penguin Books, 1976), p. 586.

[57] Wolfgang Giegerich, "Is the Soul 'Deep'?" *Spring*, 64 (1998): 19-20, and *passim*.

[58] Plotinus, *Enneads*, 6.5.12 (10); cf. *Enneads*, 6.7.12 (24).

[59] Aristotle, *De anima*, A 2.405b26-29.

INTRODUCTION

be lively (boiling)! And, for Plotinus, the hyper-boiling (*hyperzeousan*) is produced by a quality of life that is contemplative and thought-*ful* (boiling *over*, *re*flective). Surely this is why Plotinus would also say: "Men, too, when the power of contemplation [*theōrein*, "theorizing"] weakens, turn to action, a shadow [*skian*] of contemplation and reason [*theōrein kai logos*],"[60] i.e., when thinking is lacking, the soul of life is in the shadow of unconsciousness and is hardly boiling *over*![61]

The point is that thinking is a crux to realizing the dialectics of self and its soulful transformation. This is a notion that the reader of this volume may well experience as she or he begins to be engaged by the arguments of the text, as indeed were the participants in the remarkable seminar at El Capitan Canyon in California.

---

[60] Plotinus, *Enneads*, 3.8.4 (30).
[61] This is not unlike the psychological critique of "acting out" as a weak form of psychological life.

CHAPTER ONE

"Conflict/Resolution," "Opposites/Creative Union" versus Dialectics, and the Climb up the Slippery Mountain

WOLFGANG GIEGERICH

No doubt, human life is full of conflicts, conflicts between states or even entire civilizations that often lead to wars, conflicts within a society that in extreme cases may take the form of a civil war between the government and a guerrilla opposition, conflicts between as well as within institutions and companies, but also interpersonal conflicts such as in a marriage, and even conflicts within a single individual. Psychology, too, often believes that neurosis is based on "unconscious conflicts." However—quite apart from the fact that, as I see it, neurosis is not really to be understood in terms of unconscious conflicts—*at least for understanding dialectics* we have to leave the notion of "conflict" behind. It is true, conflicts, when they occur, may, like everything else, have their own internal dialectics and may develop in a dialectical fashion; they may also be the expression of a certain stage in the dialectics of political, social, personal development. But this does not mean the reverse, that dialectics could be comprehended or even defined in terms of conflict and resolution. What is wrong with the notion of "conflict" in this regard? Two things:

1. Conflict is a life phenomenon *to which* we may want to bring a dialectical understanding. What I call the "psychological difference" comes into play here: Psychology is not about life and life phenomena, not about people and their development or behavior, but it is about "the soul," the "logical life," the dialectics operative *within* such life phenomena, *within* people's behavior. With the notion of "conflicts" we are already in the outside world, in the social and empirical arena of thing-like entities and events: of human beings and their behavior, their interaction and relationships (so-called object relations), their interests, their desire and fears, and thereby we have already closed behind us the door to the sphere of "the soul"[1] and its concerns, the door to the sphere of psychology. If I may use a comparison, which of course has only limited validity, the move to psychology is like moving in physics from macrophysics to microphysics, or in biology from a concept of visible organs as the ultimate entities in the body to the invisible, irrepresentable (*unanschaulich*), abstract molecular level of genetic codes and the chemistry of protein production.

2. Dialectics does not have the *form* of conflicts and their resolution. An existing conflict is an indication that one is precisely unconscious of the dialectic and incapable of thinking dialectically and therefore has to act out the dialectic blindly, literalizing (concretizing) it. A thinking in terms of conflict positions itself in *external* reflection, in the position of an external observer. It does not look from within. A conflict implies the external collision, clash, of two opposite entities. But dialectics does not start out with opposites, and not with Two. Rather, dialectical thinking begins with one single idea, notion, phenomenon and then shows its internal contradiction. It makes one conscious of the fact that what from outside looks like a unitary and self-consistent unit is not unitary, but within itself contradicts itself. It is within itself different (distinguishing itself from itself). In this

---

[1] Note the quotation marks. Even where "the soul" in my text may not be visibly enclosed in quotation marks, the quotation marks have to be imagined, because I do not wish to posit the soul as an existing (be it metaphysical or empirical) entity or a mysterious subject. It is merely a convenient, still mythologizing (substantiating) manner of speaking. There is not a soul behind or apart from psychological phenomenology and psychological processes (which have their mercurial spirit and dynamics within themselves).

sense, dialectical thinking is *recursive*. It is neither the *intentio recta*, nor the *intentio obliqua*, but, to misappropriate a Heideggerian term for non-Heideggerian dialectical thinking, a *Schritt zurück*, a stepping backwards so as to *widen* the horizon before oneself.

A simple example for this internal self-contradiction might be the phenomenon of willing something. The will is free. The fact that we have a will is the manifestation of human freedom. This is the one side. The other side comes to the fore when we realize that willing or wanting is radically different from wishing. I can *wish* to win in the lottery, but I cannot *want* this (in the strict sense of willing) because the outcome of the lottery is totally beyond my reach. Willing always entails the will to use the real means necessary to achieve something. A person might wish to go back to school in order to get a Ph.D., but this does not necessarily mean that he or she has the will to do so. To wish such a thing might simply mean to entertain this dream in one's mind. To have the *will* to get a Ph.D., by contrast, means to be willing to give up, for several years, much free time and many weekends to spend them for studying hard while others are free to use this time for their relaxation. I am not free; I must sit down and study. In other words, the will to go back to school entails the contradiction between my free choice AND my obedience to the "must" that my choice involves. In willing, I am at once free and a slave. The will is the human capacity to be, within oneself, the unity of the unity and difference, of legislating government *and* subject bound by the laws prescribed by this government. For the everyday mind, the will is a unitary thing. That is all. It is simply one of the ultimate constituents of the human psyche. But if you open it up and look into it, you see, as in a clock, its "moving parts," its internal "engine": the inner complexity of the self-contradictory logical life that it is and *as which* it is.

This is just one small example for how in *thinking* a seemingly simple phenomenon or idea you uncover its internal dialectic. Dialectical thinking thus has a lot to do with "making conscious" and getting *inside* the topic at hand. This is why we have to uncompromisingly reject the popular misconstrual of dialectical thinking as characterized by the tripartite scheme of thesis—antithesis—synthesis. This scheme is (a) historically and philologically speaking not Hegelian, (b) in itself mindless, mechanical, unthinking, and (c) views what it calls thesis and antithesis from outside, like objects that need to be reconciled or united.

As to the first point I merely cite a few references. H. Hoppe writes: "This triple step of thesis—antithesis—s[ynthesis], which according to conventional view is supposed to characterize G. W. F. Hegel's dialectical procedure, in fact does not occur in Hegel."[2] G. E. Mueller published an article entitled, "The Hegel Legend of 'Thesis—Antithesis—Synthesis.'"[3] Terry Pinkard speaks of "the ongoing myth [...] of Hegel's system as consisting of some oddly formal triumvirate of 'Thesis, Antithesis and Synthesis' (terms that Hegel himself never uses and that also completely mischaracterize his thought)."[4] The last phrase ("mischaracterize") makes the essential point. This mischaracterization is unfortunately perpetuated by Jungians, too. In a review of my *The Soul's Logical Life*, Michael Vannoy Adams, e.g., writes, "Jung's analytical psychology and Hillman's archetypal psychology are the thesis to Giegerich's antithesis, [...]. (Whether a synthesis will emerge out of this dialectic remains to be seen)."[5] We see here very clearly how according to this understanding of dialectics you start with two givens as opposites coexisting on the same level and then hope that maybe some third might appear that resolves the conflict. The resolution is projected into the future. Dialectics is imagined as a kind of program; not totally unlike peace negotiations where you also hope for a settlement.

Another Jungian, Hester Solomon, displays in her article on "The transcendent function and Hegel's dialectical vision" [*Journal of Analytical Psychology* 39 (1994): 77-100] that she has the same misconception of Hegelian dialectics.[6] This comes out not only in her discussion of it, but also most clearly in a diagram that is supposed to represent what Hegelian dialectics is about. In this diagram (Fig. 1) we see depicted what one might call the peace negotiation fantasy about dialectics: two opponents facing each other and trying to find a common third. The only difference to peace negotiations, a difference that indeed brings it a

---

[2] H. Hoppe, "Synthesis," *Historisches Wörterbuch der Philosophie*, vol. 10 (my transl.).
[3] G. E. Mueller, "The Hegel Legend of 'Thesis – Antithesis – Synthesis,'" *Journal of the History of Ideas* 19 (1958).
[4] Terry Pinkard, *Hegel's Phenomenology* (Cambridge: Cambridge University Press, 1994), p. 17.
[5] Michael Vannoy Adams in *The Round Table Review* 6.4 (1999): 14.
[6] Hester Solomon, "The Transcendent Function and Hegel's Dialectical Vision," *Journal of Analytical Psychology* 39 (1994): 77–100.

"CONFLICT/RESOLUTION" VS. DIALECTICS

little closer to dialectics, is that Solomon speaks of a "*creative* synthesis" and depicts this as being on, or establishing, a fundamentally new level, whereas the result of peace negotiations is normally a compromise on the same old level. However, not only the idea of "two fundamental opposites" "in stagnant and mutually annihilating conflict" (p. 83), but also the idea of a longed-for "creative change" is misleading here. Hegel does not begin with opposites ("pairs of opposites," "bipolar opposites," p. 82) and does not *look for* a *creative* solution of their conflict. Rather, the process of deepening thought discovers and reveals that the opposites had been united all along in a common Ground. There is no need for a solution here, but rather the *insight* and *realization* that the experience of the opposites was due to a superficial and preliminary view. So the dialectical movement, instead of seeking a future solution, is a going under[7]; it makes explicit the presuppositions that had unwittingly been behind and inherent in one's initial assumptions; it goes back and down to the deeper Ground that had been there all the time and had merely not been seen. As we might put it in psychology, consciousness had been too unconscious, superficial, too undifferentiated, too prejudiced. The *union* of opposites (or the resolution of the contradiction) is precisely the prior reality, and a *reality* from the outset, not something to be created. What has been there from the beginning is allowed to catch up with consciousness, to come home to consciousness.

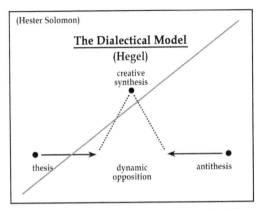

Fig. 1: Hester Solomon's Dialectical Model. The diagonal line has the function of reminding the reader that this is a false scheme.

The dialectical process does not begin with Two, but with One, with a *Position*. There is, at first, no opposition to this position, no alternatives, no "dynamic relationship" (p. 82). Rather, by committedly sticking to this one position that it holds, the mind discovers, or is

---

[7] This concurs with the idea of the "*Schritt zurück*."

forced to admit, that this position proves to be untenable. It does not hold up.

This experience amounts to a *Negation* of the initial position. If before the position was A, the negation of the position results in non-A, a contradiction to the original position. The negation, if tested, again proves to be untenable and is accordingly negated. So we get the *Negation of the Negation* (not-[non-A]). But the negation of the negation as such is *Absolute Negation* and as such the reinstitution of the original *Position* (= A). However it is now the Position on a fundamentally new level, because it is no longer the "naive" (immediate) position of the beginning, as a simple given, but *mediated* and tremendously enriched by the history of all the negations and as their net *result*. It has been greatly differentiated, is much more subtle, refined. Nothing has been lost or discarded through the negations. The superseded stages are all still there, however now only as sublated moments within the new Position. On this new level the dialectical process can then begin once more with the differentiated result as its starting point, i.e., as the new Position.

In this sense, the movement of dialectics is structurally remotely similar to that of the alchemical opus that proceeds, too, via negations. In alchemy these are of course expressed in chemical terms such as decomposition, fermenting corruption, solution, etc. In both cases the recursive process of negation is in itself and simultaneously the process of sublimating, distilling, refining the prime matter here, and consciousness or the logic of the world there. The way down into the Ground *is* dialectically the way up to a wider horizon of consciousness or a richer, more sophisticated consciousness.

Solomon's so-called dialectical model is not really dialectical at all, because it is unidirectionally about a forward move to what she calls a "creative change" and "a creative, forward moving resolution" (p. 82). It is also not really dialectic because the question *how* precisely the union of opposites comes about and what is the precise determination of the resulting Third is left open. It remains mysterious, naturally so, inasmuch as the resolution is here in the status of a longed-for future, a hope. Hegel, by contrast, *perspicuously demonstrates* how and why precisely which concrete result is produced by the dialectical movement in each case. This is so because dialectics is a work of "decomposition," "fermenting corruption,"

"CONFLICT/RESOLUTION" VS. DIALECTICS

not of constructive synthesis; it is a process of stepping backwards and going under, rather than a utopian waiting for a resolution.

What has been said about Solomon's "dialectical model" is also true about Jung's "transcendent function." It, too, is conceived by Jung as a "creative synthesis" out of an absolute fix, the tension of opposites, and here, too, *how* the creative synthesis comes about remains miraculous and what exactly it will be unforeseeable—naturally so, because Jung operates with the idea of an *un*conscious as the mysterious "author" or source *behind* the scene. For these reasons, Solomon's exactly parallel diagram for this idea of Jung's (p. 80) is perfectly adequate, *except for the fact* that she represents Jung's idea about the transcendent function as an example of Hegelian dialectics and even as a result of an alleged actual intensive study of Hegel by Jung (p. 79)[8], which does not do justice to either Hegel or Jung and, as far as the latter is concerned, is in blatant conflict with Jung's own assertion that he "never studied Hegel properly, that means his original works. There is no possibility of inferring a direct dependence […]." "In the intellectual world in which I grew up, Hegelian thought played no role at all; […] Hegel's dialectics, I can safely say, had no influence at all, as far as I know myself" (*Letters 2*, 501f., to Rychlak, 27 April 1959). Indeed, Jung adamantly rejected Hegel, and his "transcendent function" is an idea of the polar tension, even collision, of opposites. His thinking here is, as it were, inspired by physics, electronics, as the following statement (also quoted by Solomon, p. 81) shows: "The confrontation of the two positions generates a tension charged with energy and creates a living, third thing … a living birth that leads to a new level of being, a new situation" (*CW* 8 § 189). This is a *naturalistic*, positivistic thinking. Also, Jung's standpoint is that of an external observer: The two opposites are conceived from outside as positive facts, like two things or physical forces. Their dynamic interaction and its result, a solution, is conceived as a factual, irrational *event*, something that simply happens one way or another. Jung does not try to get into the process and view it from within in its internal consistency. The external, physical imagination comes out most clearly when Jung imagines the experience of the opposites as the subject's being between hammer and anvil, or as its being torn in opposite directions.

---

[8] Cf. also: "… Jung's concept of the transcendent function derives its philosophical basis from the notion of dialectical change, first expounded by … Hegel…" (p. 77).

Hegel's dialectical thinking, by contrast, proceeds from the standpoint of interiority. The original "Position" is not thing-like, but linguistic, a proposition, thesis, an idea, i.e., it is seen from the outset as something noetic, as belonging to the mind. And the process also continues linguistically and rationally via negation or contra*diction* and leads to an *inherent* logical consequence (not an irrational event as the result of a conflict between natural forces). Using as an image the fact that books can be used for two fundamentally different types of purposes, *either*, e.g., for weighing down freshly glued paper, as a support under a table leg to stabilize the table, as a weapon to be thrown at somebody's head, etc., *or* for *reading*, in other words, *either* as a dead object *or* as a door to the mental world, Jung's idea of the confrontation of the two opposites could be likened to the collision of two closed books, while the dialectical procedure would have to be said to work with an open book, i.e., with the thought that is its content, a thought that consecutively evokes a contradiction, and thus a new book to be written, and so on.

After these rather abstract-formal comments on the difference between dialectics and thinking in terms of conflict and opposition, I want to illustrate, with the help of a concrete example, how dialectical thinking works. I will start out with a short dream of a patient, relate its main motif to ancient imaginal material (fairy tale, myth) and show three things: (1) that ancient imaginal texts, while not themselves being exemplars of thought proper, nevertheless portray by imaginal or narrative means what is actually a dialectical relation and movement; (2) that in order to do justice to these texts, it is our job to approach them with a dialectically thinking and comprehending mind so as to make their implicit dialectic explicit; and (3) that the point of the dialectical movement is to interiorize into absolute negativity and thus into the standpoint of the soul.

But first a personal comment. I find that often people try to make me a Hegelian, simply because I refer to Hegel and have learned a few things from him. But neither do I propagate Hegel's philosophy, nor do I claim that what I say is such that Hegel would have been of one mind with me. I do not even claim to understand Hegel properly. My work is in psychology and about our modern situation, and is not an attempt to propound Hegel's philosophy. Our purpose in our time cannot be to inscribe our modern psychological interests and needs into the ready-made form of Hegel's system and to rely on him as an authority that validates our own work. We have to think from within our own historical situation and on our own responsibility. *However*, I think that in trying to do so there is no way around Hegel. It is the most advanced, comprehensive, and differentiated thinking and supersedes everything that came afterwards (including deconstructive thinking, which is, compared with Hegel, systematically one-sided). In Hegel, an intellectual level has been reached and a standard been set to fall short of which our thought cannot afford. It will never do not to come up to the state of the art that "the soul" in its history has already reached. But quite apart from this generally valid observation, the specific indispensability of Hegel for psychology (i.e., psychology as the discipline of interiority and interiorization) is that there is no other body of thought that could better initiate into, and train in, absolute negativity, interiority, and the capacity to "uroborically" ("speculatively") comprehend the other as the soul's/the (sentence) subject's own other.

The Climb Up the Slippery Mountain

Let us suppose that a woman in the middle of her life reports during her first therapy session the following dream, that she has had repeatedly.

> I am trying to climb up a mountain. Although there is a well-paved slope beside me, I am walking on sandy ground. For every step I take forward, I slip down two steps backward.

Dreams with this motif of the slippery mountain are not rare. But this particular dream is very special in that it offers two alternative options. The dream-ego could easily walk on the well-paved part where she would not have any problem. But the dream makes her try, without the least hesitation, to climb the mountain on the slippery part, where she necessarily experiences frustration and failure. Since from the point of view of the reality principle such behavior would be absurd, it must be "the soul" and not the ego that has an interest in submitting the dream-ego to this experience of continuously trying hard and continuously failing. The point seems to be to commit consciousness to a fundamentally "impossible" task. This utterly bewildering theme obviously does not make sense in terms of the pragmatics of everyday life and the human or ego concern for survival (survival in the widest sense of the word). It confronts the dreamer and us with totally different concerns.

We know the commitment to impossible tasks from myths about the underworld. Think of the tale of Sisyphus, who had to roll a heavy rock up a mountain, a rock that time and again rolled back down shortly before the summit was reached. In the historically late reports about these underworld mythemes, the pointlessness of these tasks is usually explained as a punishment by the gods for some outrage. Wherever such a moral interpretation occurs, we can be certain that a later (post-mythological) age no longer understood the original initiatory meaning and used its own incompatible categories of guilt and punishment to make sense of it. So we have to reconstruct the earlier meaning. The Sisyphus myth, being reduced to one simple image, is too abbreviated for this purpose. We find our dream motif in a more extended form in the fairy tales of the type AT[9] 530, "The Princess On the Glass Mountain." More than 300 variant versions from many countries of this fairytale type have come down to us, the oldest example being in an Egyptian text from the second millennium B.C.E. I basically follow the Norwegian tale.

> The fairy tale has two distinct parts. In the first part we hear of a peasant who has three sons. Every year during a certain night just before it is time to make hay the grass from his meadows is radically eaten off as if by a huge herd of animals. The man sends his sons, one at a time each year, to guard the meadow during this night, but the older two sons fall asleep and only the youngest one, a dimwit, stays awake and finds that the perpetrator is a huge copper-colored horse, on which there was fastened a complete knight's armor of shiny copper. He manages to catch the horse and leaves it at a secret place with someone for safekeeping. In the two following years he acquires in the same way two additional horses, one silvery with a knight's armor of silver, one golden with an armor of gold.
>
> In the second half, a king wants to marry off his daughter. He sets her on top of a glass mountain. He announces: Any man

---

[9] AT refers to the standard international classification of fairy tales: Antti Aarne and Stith Thompson, *The Types of the Folktale* (= Folklore Fellows Communications No. 184), 2nd Revision, Helsinki 1981. (Based on Antti Aarne's *Verzeichnis der Märchentypen* [FF Communications No. 3] 1910.

who can ride up to her and take the three golden apples from her lap will receive her as his wife and will inherit the kingdom. On the day set everyone, except the dimwit, who is told to stay at home, tries his luck. But the mountain is so slippery that no one succeeds. At the end of the day when they want to give up in desperation, there appears from the distance a knight in a shiny copper armor on a copper-colored horse and effortlessly manages to ride up the glass mountain. But after he is one third up, he turns around and disappears again. But the princess had been so enchanted when seeing him that she had rolled down to him one of her golden apples. On the next day, when all want to go home in the evening in frustration, a knight in silver armor appears and rides two thirds up the mountain and, after receiving the second apple, disappears again. On the third day a knight in golden armor appears and rides up the whole mountain, takes the third apple from the lap of the princess and disappears unrecognized again. The king orders all the men of his whole kingdom to appear before him in order to find the man who has the three apples, and in the end our dimwit is summoned. He produces the apples and reveals himself in his golden armor. He marries the princess and receives half the kingdom.

The first half of our tale and many details of the second half, as important and interesting as they may be, are of no concern to us here. We concentrate exclusively on the one motif of the task of riding up the slippery mountain and on both the failure and the success in doing so. And I will not look at this motif with a view to finding out what it and the other rich symbolism of this whole fairy tale may have meant in the ages when the tale was invented (at least a few millennia ago) and in the context of the archaic psyche and ritualistic life. I use (maybe abuse) it only for our own purpose of illustrating *dialectical interiorization into absolute negativity*.

The first thing to note is that, by setting the king's daughter on top of a glass mountain, i.e., not an ordinary geographical mountain, but the primordial metaphysical mountain connecting the world with heaven, the fairy tale shows that she is out of this world, in the beyond. This is in keeping with all "genuine fairy tales," those tales that are "tales of magic" (*Zaubermärchen*). In them, the princess sought by the human hero represents an otherworldly, non-human being, a figure belonging to the transcendent world of spirits and fairies. So the desire and love of the man for the princess involves us in the theme of a fundamentally asymmetrical relationship across a barrier between "species" or "categories." This fact lends itself to pointing again to the "psychological difference." The fairy tale shows us that the soul's interest is not in our human, interpersonal relationships, relationships between man and woman, nor in the sexes or in gender issues. Such topics belong in the social sphere and are psychologically irrelevant. The soul's interest, by contrast, is in how to cross the border from here (from the human, all-too-human or empirical side) to the beyond. Only he can become king who is capable of actually getting there and back again, bringing back into this world the treasure from there. And because it is a veritable transgression from here to the other world, we have in our tale the image of the slippery glass mountain.

In terms of formal reflection, the king and the task set by him of riding up the mountain can be considered the *Position*. The Position is: you can ride up the glass mountain; or more specifically: you can ride from this earth to the transcendent heaven. The king is the living proof of the Position, inasmuch as in fairy tales to be king, i.e., shaman, means nothing else but the capacity to reach transcendence; kingship in fairy tales is not a political office.

The slipperiness of the mountain, i.e., the impossibility of achieving this goal, is the *Negation*.

Now, if the two older brothers and all the other men of the kingdom do not let themselves be deterred by their constantly slipping down, but for three days all day long try their best to nevertheless fulfill the task, then this amounts to the *Negation of the Negation*. At any rate, through their failure despite their absolutely devoted attempts the idea of being able to go from here to the beyond just like that, by ordinary human means, is beyond any doubt proven to be impossible. By trying so hard, with total commitment, to climb up and slipping back time and again, the original assumption is exhaustively tried, but revealed to be an illusion, and the disillusionment is unrelentingly inscribed into consciousness.

However, the story does not stop there. The suddenly appearing anonymous, mysterious knight in his shiny metal armor, by demonstrating that the task can be done after all, brings the *Absolute Negation*, which amounts to an affirmation.

And, to finish this brief outline about the four stages of formal reflection, the dimwit brother by revealing himself in the end as the one who fetched the golden apples from yonder, and by marrying the princess and becoming the new king, represents the *Restored Position*.

It is clear that this sequence of stages can be found in the fairy tale. But it might not fully convince us as a plausible depiction of the logical stages of reflection, since the Absolute Negation becomes possible only miraculously, through magical means, which is acceptable for a fairy tale, but not for a logical development. Therefore we have to make a distinction here between what is due to the imagistic and narrative *form* of the story, on the one hand, and how what is depicted in this narrative form is to be comprehended if it is truly thought, on the other. The narrative form has, above all, three problems. It represents as action in time, as a sequence of events, what actually, that is, logically, occurs all at once—different internal moments of one reality, namely the one reality of successfully reaching transcendence from this earth. Secondly, the narrative embodies abstract logical stages of reflection in separate figures, as if they were individual people with their own personalities, characters, actions, and motivations. Thereby it, thirdly, creates the impression that the failure of the two older brothers and all the other men on the one hand, and the success of the unknown knight on the other, were separate, independent events, whereas in truth they are inherently connected, the one being the consistent logical *result* of the other. This needs to be shown.

An important question is why in our tale, as in so many other fairy tales, there are three brothers, two older clever ones, who, however, fail, and one younger dimwit, who successfully manages to cross over into the realm of transcendence. The introduction of the failing brothers cannot merely be a literary device to give, through the contrast with their failure, all the more profile and glory to the miraculous achievement of the youngest son. We have to realize that the three brothers are not simply a series of three, three brothers side by side and of equal standing. All these fairy tales with three brothers show much rather that we have the formal relationship of 2 + 1, i.e., the two older ones are really brothers to each other in a human, empirical sense and belong exclusively to the realm of positivity or ordinary life, while the youngest son is of a dual nature, *utriusque capax*, as the alchemists might have said. He has a positive side, too, to be sure, but it is not the important one, not fully developed.

Living in the world of positivity he nevertheless actually, and more deeply, belongs somewhere else. *This* is the reason why he is called a dimwit and why he is consistently excluded from joining all the rest of the people competing for the princess. He is *a priori* singled out, sequestered from the rest. This is reminiscent of the fact that in ritualistic cultures certain individuals were removed from the ordinary life of the community, declared as "sacred" and as such raised and reserved for the sole purpose of some day, in times of a predicament, serving a specific ritual purpose, e.g., as the sacrificial victim to be ritually slaughtered for the boon of the community in a particular rite necessitated by this predicament. The youngest son, by being sequestered, is given a status ontologically or logically different from that of his brothers and all the other men. He is meant to be of an entirely different order. His strength, destination and life-task lie somewhere else: they come to light in the shining knight. What is he, if he is not one of them? He is the Third of the Two, which is about the same thing as what the quintessence is for the Four.

This insight entails an important consequence: seen logically, i.e., if we leave the mode of mental picturing behind and *think* what is happening here, the efforts of the older brothers and the achievement of the youngest brother are not independent of each other, separate parallel attempts concerning the same task with different outcomes. They are connected, indeed strictly "identical," but dialectically so. Without his older brothers, the younger one—at least to the extent that he is the golden knight—would not exist at all; without the total failure of the two brothers at riding up the mountain, the golden knight could not appear. Their *failure* is the indispensable precondition of his *success*. But not only that. Rather, his success merely brings out into the open what their failure intrinsically is.

As I pointed out, the particular failure of the two brothers represents not only the Negation, but is in itself also the Negation of the Negation. In order to understand how this is so, we must again not merely stay in the imagining, mental-picturing mode, but *think* what is happening to the two brothers and all their fellow combatants at the slippery mountain. Single-mindedly they persist all day long in trying to move *up* the mountain—and persistently they slide *down*. By showing us this, the narrative represents in imagistic terms the self-contradictory dialectic of one single movement, a movement which is continuously

"CONFLICT/RESOLUTION" VS. DIALECTICS 15

and at one and the same time an upward *and* a downward movement. If it is both at once, what does this mean, and what does it *do to* the movement? Because the movement persists and yet is simultaneously counteracted, *the upward movement slides, as it were, into itself*. It is forced back into *itself*; in logical terminology: it is reflected into itself. It is interiorized, not into the person trying to move up, not into his interior, but interiorized into itself.

The upward movement is not simply stopped. The men do not give up, do not simply turn around and go back home in frustration, having concluded from their experience that this is an impossible and therefore pointless undertaking. This would be the simple Negation of the upward move. No, they stay at it, as Sisyphus does, thereby exemplifying the statement by Hegel: "But the life of the Spirit is not the life that shrinks from death and keeps itself untouched by devastation, but rather the life that endures it and maintains itself in it."[10] The upward movement is in this sense not canceled by the Negation, not given up altogether; it maintains itself in its being negated and in this sense is the negation of the negation. The upward move sort of says to itself: "Never mind the slipping down, do not succumb to the negation, *but* do not avoid it, shrink from it, protect yourself from it, either. Rather expose yourself to it unrelentingly, allowing it to do its work upon you."

What concretely does "negation of the negation" mean here? Because the slipping down, i.e., the negation, is itself negated, it does not undo the upward movement altogether or as such. The latter precisely maintains itself despite being negated. It stays a progression, a forward move. However, it does not maintain itself unscathed in its former form either, but only *as* negated. The movement, rather than being negated by a force from outside, has become negative *to itself* and within itself, in other words, self-contradictory: a *recursive progression*. It has been thoroughly baptized or soaked in negativity and permeated with it. In alchemical language: it has been putrefied, fermented, and corrupted, but *ipso facto* also sublimated, distilled, vaporized, become spiritual.[11] Thus, what the negation negated is

---

[10] G. W. F. Hegel, *Phenomenology of Spirit*, translated by A.V. Miller (Oxford: Oxford University Press, 1977), p. 19.
[11] "Spiritual" of course not in the lofty sense of spiritual practices, in the sense of Hillman's distinction between "peaks" versus "vales." But in the (let's say) alchemical sense (the mercurial spirit in matter, e.g.).

only the literalistic, external, positive, empirical-factual *understanding* of a progressing to the beyond, the whole *spatial* imagining of moving up or down. External and extensional space is left behind altogether; by forcing the movement into *itself*, the negation of the negation of the forward movement creates and opens up for the experiencing mind a totally new and unexpected dimension, a no-space, a logically negative "space," the intensional space of interiority or "the soul," of true and real transcendence, which is true and real because it is no longer imagined as a positivity out there, in the beyond (or, for that matter, as a positivity in ourselves, our "inner," in the beyond of our "unconscious").

Transcendence, interiority, or "the soul" do not exist as a positive reality. They are not a special part or region of the empirical world. They come about only *through a logical act*, through the *negation* of externality, of space as such, which negation in turn is possible only through the negation or self-contradiction of a passionately attempted forward movement. The move into transcendence being absolute-negative is not a soaring higher and higher up beyond the earth and beyond the clouds into outer space. On the contrary, since it is negative (frustrated) movement, it stays put.

Now we are in a position to answer the question why the mountain has to be slippery and how the negation of the Position comes about in the first place. So far I have treated the slipping down as an additional, new event, independent of the task set by the king. But now we have to realize that it is intrinsic to this task itself. The Negation of the Position is not something that simply happens to the Position from outside, a contingent circumstance, such as a prohibition or an obstacle. No, it evolves from the Position itself. It is its own doing, its self-negation. The task set is the ascent into transcendence. If the ascent were successful, the sons would reach the mountain top, but then this mountain top would *ipso facto* be an ordinary mountain top in the empirical world and they would not have entered transcendence. Even if they had spaceships and could fly to the farthest spiral nebulae in outer space, they would still be in the ordinary physical world. This is the internal dialectic of the Position, of the initial task set by the king: if the upward movement were simply possible and successful, it would fail; precisely its success would be its failure. And this, not the slipping down, is the true Negation of the Position. In order to truly ascend to transcendence, the movement must not simply go on and on and on *ad infinitum* (the "bad infinity" of the infinite progress), it must not be acted out. Going on and on, it would never transcend, never transgress, it would conversely affirm the continuous extent of empirical-factual reality. Transcendence is not a (special, distant) *place* in empirical reality.

Therefore, so that there can be a transgression into transcendence, the very *notion* of ascension has to *be applied to itself*. And this self-application of the notion of moving up results in a negation. For inasmuch as the climbing does no longer merely climb up some external other, a mountain out there, but climbs up *itself* (the very Notion of climbing), the climbing movement climbs beyond literal climbing or ascending, transcends it, sublates it; it leaves behind the idea of a simple, ordinary forward movement in space. The upward move is *er-innert* (interiorized) into itself, which opens up the wholly other dimension of interiority in the first place. And this, nothing else, *is* the transgression into transcendence, inasmuch as in this way the world of positivity and the acting out in external or empirical space are indeed overcome. And this interiorization of the Notion of climbing into itself is also what is pictorially expressed in our tale by the simultaneity of trying to move forward and slipping back down.

Generally speaking, in methodological terms, the dialectic proceeds via the self-application of the notion or category that happens to be at stake in each case. Why this self-application? With the simple application (the application to other items outside and in front of itself) the concept or category would merely be acted out. But it must also be *er-innert*, come home to itself. Physician, heal thyself, take your own medicine. The concept must not remain aloof, itself exempt from and above the sphere of its jurisdiction.

To the extent that the upward movement is, as it were, a slipping down into itself, the goal of the movement, the mountain top and the princess upon it, logically "slip down" into it, too, and are negatively interiorized into the movement itself. For this reason the elder brothers' failure to get up to the princess on the mountaintop in the literal spatial sense *is* the success of reaching her and reaching the transcendent *in truth*, because "the princess" or the transcendent *is* nothing else but the space of interiority that is opened up, exclusively opened up, through the interiorization of the goal of the movement into the movement itself, thereby overcoming the positive (or positivistic) understanding of transcendence. The movement having turned in on itself now has everything it needs within itself, even its own goal, the princess (who of course is not to be taken as a real person, but merely as a symbolic embodiment of "transcendence" or "the land of the soul"). The climbing movement has its goal no longer outside and ahead of the movement, as something to long for. In this sense the slipping back of the upward movement into itself *is* the true reaching of the goal, the only true reaching there is.

So the two elder brothers did not fail at all. Rather, it is precisely in their "failure" that the elder brothers succeed. They manage to get up the mountain to the princess, only not in positivity, not on the level of acted out literal behavior (where the princess and transcendence could not be found anyway), and not they as ego. No, they manage it in negativity, "in Mercurio," as the alchemists might have said.

And this *their* mercurial, *absolute-negative* success is then in our fairy tale pictorially brought out into the open and objectified in a separate image, namely as the miraculous apparition of the shining knight who effortlessly rides up the mountain. Rather than being one of the competitors alongside the other knights and his brothers, he is indeed something like the "quintessence" or the image of the inner truth of the absolute-negative interiorization of the forward move into itself. Contrary to how it appears in the narrative, the appearance of the knight is not a new event in addition to the other people's upward movement's slipping back down into itself. The miraculous knight is no more than *its* further-determination, the unfolding and manifestation of its inner essence: the explicit revelation of the Negation of the Negation as in itself being Absolute Negativity.

The reason why the success of the older brothers has to be shown as the success of an other and as a distant and absolutely miraculous apparition of the copper, silver, golden knight clearly set off from, and remaining totally anonymous for them is, first, that it is a non-ego success, a success in Absolute Negativity, and secondly that with a fairy tale we are of course in a medium where Absolute Negativity cannot yet be *thought*, but has to be represented imagistically. The brothers' success is not positive success and not theirs as ego-personalities. In *myths*, the absolute negativity of impossible tasks, such as the one Sisyphus has to perform, is expressed by their being portrayed as occurring in the *underworld*.

In a psychologistic, still positivistic imagining of these fairytale events we might conceive of them in the following way. The brothers, by exhausting themselves all day in monotonously trying to move up and slipping down, worked themselves up into a trance, and in this trance, i.e., in a visionary experience, they beheld the visionary fulfillment of their own endeavors. But we should use this fantasy only as a bridge, a *pons asinorum*, that needs to be burned behind us right after our having crossed it. It is not adequate. For there is no literal trance, no literal visionary apparition, nothing experiential or emotional. What there is is the *notional* truth of the intensional space of interiority or the successful "initiation" of consciousness into transcendence or Absolute Negativity, where "initiation" means entering into a sphere or "space" that is produced or realized only through one's entering it absolutely-negatively, i.e., a space that without this entering *would not exist at all*. An initiation *produces* that into which it leads in the first place. The awareness of Absolute Negativity has to be notional, logical, occur in thought, because it does not exist outside of thought.

Why does the knight who can miraculously ride up to the mountaintop have to disappear unrecognized and unidentified? For the simple reason that he is only in the status of an apparition in absolute negativity. As such he lacks a positive existence and therefore cannot hold his place in reality yet. Just as you cannot, just like that, ride up the glass mountain, you cannot either, just like that, bring back into ordinary reality the golden apples from their own realm, the realm of absolute negativity. An additional and final step is necessary in the fairy tale. It begins discontinuously, after a rupture, and now from within the realm of positivity, with real, empirical persons, not with figures in the sphere of negativity, and particularly with the youngest son in his positively real existence in contrast to his deeper nature as the mysterious knight.

How can the gain inherent in a real acquisition of the notion of absolute negativity make itself felt in positive reality? Those who have undergone absolute-negative interiorization and thus entered "the land of the soul" must, as real persons, be distinguishable from the others, who are without access to "the soul" or Absolute Negativity. The experience of having been there must in some way leave its mark on the empirical person, who will in practical life probably react to the same things somewhat differently from others—more deeply, subtly, more soulfully—and will probably also have a different presence, perhaps even a charisma. Despite being absolutely negative and thus hidden, it must somehow show in ordinary reality, too. Who the person is who is in possession of the boon is determined in the last step of the fairy tale. And by finally determining this person, it becomes apparent what Absolute Negativity has already implicitly been all along: the Restored Position, imagistically speaking: the new king.

We might think that the third son, inasmuch as he is in possession of the golden apples, would immediately after his return have presented them, revealed himself, and claimed the promised reward. But this is not the case. On the contrary, the old king has to summon all the people in his kingdom in order to laboriously *search out* the right person from among them. Why is this so? Because if the youngest son had tried to present his apples to his family and neighbors and to reveal himself to them, they would not have been able to recognize the golden apples as the boon from yonder, and they would also have been blind to the golden shine of his armor or rather his person. *They* can see only the plain and ordinary, only the dimwit. *Aurum nostrum non est aurum vulgi*, the alchemists said. The golden apples are not a positivity, not empirical-factual proof that will convince Everyman and can, so to speak, stand up in court. The boon being absolute-negative, the youngest son has nothing to *show* that would support his claim. Rather, he is entirely dependent on being *detected*, on being *seen* in his deeper truth as the golden knight, *by him* who in his time had also managed to ride up the glass mountain and had received *his* golden apples. For only like can know like. Only the old king is capable of recognizing his equal and recognizing him *through* his external, human, all-too-human appearance.

Just like the persistent effort of moving up is negatively interiorized into itself, so a logical interpretation must realize that this story is not really about different persons, subjects. *The real and only subject is the movement of the reflection itself*, and the persons appearing in the narrative have to be subjected to Negation and to the Negation of the Negation, too. They have to be distilled, so that we can realize that they are no more than the pictorial visualizations of the different moments of this movement, the old king *metonymically* representing the Position, the older brothers (the Negation as well as) the Negation of the Negation, the coppery, silvery, and golden knight Absolute Negation, and the new king the Restored Position. The glass mountain and the princess on top embody the realm of absolute negativity or the land of the soul. Earlier, I stated that the upward movement, interiorized into itself, has everything it needs within itself. This also includes the persons. They, too, have to be seen, or rather thought, as interiorized into the movement, which is *the only remaining real subject*, the Objective Subject. All substance, all entities, all subjective subjects have to be comprehended as having been vaporized and integrated as sublated moments into the self-contradictory climbing movement. Only when we can comprehend the persons, too, as sublated moments within the Objective Subject, i.e., within the logical motion, do we really view the fairy tale from the standpoint of interiority, i.e., psychology.

This logical motion, however, is not happening "out there," *at* the glass mountain. It is not a sequence of *events*, not a story, an adventure. No, it is a movement "in here," in the *comprehending* mind, in thought: in the thought of the one single concept of "transcendence." It is the problem of fairy tales that through their form they seduce us into projecting that which is actually a movement in thought (in our thinking) out of the interiority of the mind into the externality of (imagined) time and space and thus translating it into an action, an action *in front of* the mind that we merely seem to *witness* when hearing the tale. We have to resist this temptation and recall the action of the tale back into the mind so that we can use the seeming action of the fairy tale merely as a kind of visual aid for thinking the concept of transcendence, much like an abacus can be used to help us to perform the mental act of calculating.

In itself, the movement in the story is just the self-unfolding of the internal determinations of the one concept "transcendence" or absolute negativity. Instead of using the word "transcendence" mindlessly, merely as a label or a signifier, like a marker in a board game, the fairy tale spells out *what* one is saying when one is using it, *what* the complex dialectical movement is that the mind has to go through in order to form this concept and that is now collapsed into the one word "transcendence." This concept is never left in our tale; we do not move, as in an adventure story, from one event or situation to another. The movement does not bring anything new, that has not been there all along. The fairy tale is tautegorical throughout. Whether (to stay with the *imagery* of our fairy tale) you say merely the one word "glass mountain" or whether you say "climbing and slipping back" or "mysterious successful knight"—you always say the same thing, "transcendence." Each moment of the movement represents the whole concept, the whole dialectic, although only in one particular (limited) way, from one particular angle: the princess represents the absolute truth as absolutely out of reach, the tale shows the positive effort as being utterly negated, the absolute-negative success as totally irrepresentable in empirical reality and the dimwit as seen through as the true king or shaman. Each moment has *its* appropriate negation with itself and thus is *perfect* in itself.

Because Albert Camus did not make the step beyond personalistic and existentialist prejudice, the prejudice that the subjective subject is the only and the real subject, his great intuition about the *Myth of Sisyphus* had to be *An essay about the absurd*, and he got stuck in an interpretation of Sisyphus's activity as a stubborn revolt against the meaninglessness of existence for the egoic purpose of self-realization.

To return to the dream that I started out with, we see there that one and the same mountain appears, so to speak, as two essentially different mountains, or that there can be two fundamentally different perceptions of the task of climbing the mountain. With its well-paved slope, the mountain is seen as a mountain in ordinary empirical reality, and the bad dialectic of climbing such a mountain is that, to be sure, you can, just like that, successfully climb up to its top, but that, alas!, where you get to is not where you wanted and were meant to go. You went through the trouble of climbing, but your climbing did not make you transcend ordinary reality, the realm of positivity, and reach the beyond, the land of the soul, or the princess. With the perception of the mountain as a well-paved slope, there is no sense whatsoever of a negation; the mind stays totally positivistic. We could also say that in this stance the negation itself, and as such, is what is here *a priori* negated (excluded, exiled), prior to the task of climbing having been set, so that the climbing cannot be subjected to a negation of the negation and inevitably stays contained in the realm of positivity.

"CONFLICT/RESOLUTION" VS. DIALECTICS

But with its slippery part, the mountain is perceived as "the glass mountain," with which "the soul" sets itself the task of reaching out for, and *in fact* reaching, the princess/transcendence/heaven/the beyond/the dimension of soul.

Nevertheless, vis-à-vis this task, three additional, fundamentally different stances that also miss the point are possible. Two of them are different stances of refusing to accept or avoiding the challenge altogether, and the third is accepting the challenge, but checkmating it. In them there is a clear, all too powerful sense of the negative, but the negation is literally acted out, not remembered, interiorized.

First, you can say that it is absolutely impossible to reach transcendence, so that to attempt to climb the glass mountain would be futile from the outset and thus simply a foolish misunderstanding, or that to try to do so might even be thought of as absolutely forbidden, as hubris. The beyond is here *emphatically, literally* beyond, projected out and away somewhere high up there and imagined *as a positivity* (a positivity, however, that is different from other positivities in that it is defined as unreachable, though this is of course self-contradictory. The negation here has the form of an exiling, outlawing of the goal). This is the main attitude of traditional religions as popularly understood, and in personal experience it often manifests itself as resignation, as metaphysically having given up, or, more positively, in the mode of worship and upward looking, of longingly dreaming of the venerated, unreachable ideal, the thing-in-itself, or whatever it may be called.

Secondly, you can say, in "sour grapes" style, that the idea of there being a princess at the top of the mountain is just rubbish. There *is* no such thing as the soul or paradise or heaven. It is an illusion, superstition, a mystification. There is only the empirical-factual world with its pragmatic concerns, psychologically only the social arena and its personalistic or ego concerns. This is the attitude of skepticism and cynicism. Negation here has the form of devaluation and wholesale dismissal of the goal, i.e., a denial that it is a worthwhile goal.

The third type of defense is that of psychologizing this whole topic, that is to say, of conceiving it as an emotional or existential experience in one's, or from one's, unconscious. There *is* a sense here of what the challenge actually amounts to and involves: an interiorization of the goal, but the interiorizing is itself positivized and acted out as a literal behavior or event. Here, the very heart of the challenge is seen and empirically accepted, but only by logically doing it in and rendering it pointless. The psychologistic approach is the most sophisticated defense because it subverts the absolute-negative interiorization from within, reverting it into the opposite. Absolute-negative interiorization is changed into the positive "inner" or "unconscious" in us, and the movement character of the dialectic is changed into emotion and static contents, as food or stimulation for one's emotions (the feeling-experience of archetypal images), and the logical or thought character of the soul's life is reduced to the behavior of imagining.

If, however, you really accept the challenge that the soul sets with the slippery mountain, neither avoiding the challenge by acting out the negation, nor by positivizing the challenge into an ordinary pragmatic mountaineering job, nor by literally interiorizing the interiorization, then it will interiorize, not you, but your upward movement absolutely-negatively deeper and deeper into itself and *ipso facto* open up the dimension of transcendence or the land of the soul. How else could one reach transcendence? We already know that transcendence or "the soul" is nothing that positively exists. There is not such a thing as "the soul" or as transcendence. It is not out there somewhere as a place, a region or realm, a force, in short not as a literal reality. It is essentially performative. It needs to be produced, but of course produced not as a positive reality. It *is* only in and as absolute negativity, as the result of a negation plus the ensuing negation of the negation, that is to say, it is only *when, to the extent that, and for as long as* a passionate commitment to get to it is neither simply acted out, nor *simply* negated, but rather dialectically, absolutely-negatively, interiorized into itself.

CHAPTER TWO

"Different Moments of Truth"— A Few Examples

WOLFGANG GIEGERICH

From Kant we know the distinction between "synthetic judgments" and "analytic judgments." In the latter, the predicate tells you what is already implicitly contained in the subject, e.g., "all bodies are extended," while in synthetic judgments the predicate gives you some new information beyond what is implied by the concept of the subject, such as "some bodies are heavy." You cannot think a body that would not be extended (three-dimensional), but we can think bodies that are of little or even without weight (such as the ones in geometry). So the notion of "body" necessarily entails the notion of extension, but it does not entail the notion of weight. The attribute of heaviness would be an addition.

In my previous paper on dialectics I discussed briefly the phenomenon or concept of the will. What I said about it would have to be understood as analytic statements in the sense just given. I showed what "willing" involves; I unfolded, or took apart, the internal complexities of what is collapsed into one notion when we simply say,

"I will." In a similar way, I approach myths and related stories. I see in them an analysis or explication of one single concept in each case, the concept or notion of one life situation or phenomenon, one truth, one archetypal reality, only that this analysis or explication is presented in imagistic and narrative form. One may be reminded here of Bachofen's dictum that myth is the exegesis of the symbol. Inasmuch as my reading of myth is a psychological one and I define psychology as the discipline of interiority, my thinking about myth obviously has to be analytic in this sense. It cannot be synthetic, because if it were synthetic, I would think of something that has something literally outside of itself, a literal Other, and then it *ipso facto* would be a thinking in terms of *external* relations between two or more things or persons. But for psychology there is no Other. Or the other that there is is "the soul's" own other, its internal other, that is to say, itself *as* other. "The soul" is self-relation. It has nothing outside of itself. And conversely, if we think in terms of an other truly outside and vis-à-vis, of a relation literally between two, e.g., of "object relations," "interpersonal relations," of a "conflict between opposites," etc., we have left psychology. We then are in the physical world, in external reality, in the social world of real people, but no longer in the world of soul.

In the last part of *The Soul's Logical Life* I demonstrated this type of reading myth. I claimed that the Actaion-Artemis myth is about what we today have to call the rigorous notion of psychology and tried to show what this involves. I read this myth as the "analytic" unfolding, in pictorial form, of the internal complexities, the living dialectic, of the standpoint of psychology. Psycho-logy (the logos of/about the soul) is that one of the soul's moments of truth in which the soul wants to know itself (the naked truth about itself). And this knowing in the Actaion myth shows itself not to be a static fact, but in itself a complex logical motion with several stages and internal reversals. With an inappropriate technical analogy, we could say that if psychology were a car, then the myth shows us what is under the hood and how its motor works. Actaion and Artemis are not two beings, not, as subject and object, literal others. Rather, it is the soul as Actaion that encounters *itself* as Artemis and slowly is forced to realize that the logic of this encounter, the logic of true knowing, the logic of that particular moment of truth which is about the *event* (or explicit factual experience) of truth itself (of "the soul's" beholding itself unveiled, in its *nuda veritas*), does away with the initial seeming difference between the two.

So I use the term "truth" in two different senses; in the one sense ("moments of truth") it is syntactic, while in the other ("event of truth") semantic (the specific content of this event happens to be that of true knowing, whereas other events have other contents, i.e., make aware of other "moments of truth," Jung might have said other archetypes). As to the first sense, it is necessary to note that the soul's truths do not receive their truth character from anywhere else—in contrast to our usual concept of truth, which is about the correspondence between our propositions or opinions and the real facts and as such fundamentally comparative, questionable, in need of justification. Since they are the soul's truths, these truths are primordial, irreducible, "archetypal." They have their measure *within themselves*, indeed, they *are* the measure for, or the ground (in a metaphysical sense) of, what can be empirically experienced as true. They are thus "not what the eye can see, but what opens the eye" (*Kena Upanishad*). Artemis in the Actaion myth, by contrast, as the *semantic* image of the naked truth, represents the truth precisely as "what the eyes can (and need to) see."

In the story of the slippery mountain that I discussed earlier with a view to elucidating what interiorization into absolute negativity is, we have a similar concern to the one in the Actaion myth, the soul (in the form of the three brothers) striving to get to itself as the otherworldly princess on top of the glass mountain. But making the effort to climb is not hunting and killing, and sliding down is not being changed into a stag. This story is not about the soul's desire to know itself, not about that moment or truth of itself in which the soul wants to know its own unveiled truth and to assimilate the subject to the object; rather it is about another truth, the very different moment of the soul's need to gain access to the land of the soul and to bring soulfulness from yonder across a fundamental border into this, the empirical world. This is why we have the clear separation here between the mysterious appearance of the golden knight and the empirical-factual recognition of the youngest brother as the possessor of the golden apples. Here the soul wants to realize itself amidst this world, that is, to ensoul this empirical-factual world, enrich it with its own depth, its golden radiance. Whereas for that moment of the soul's truth in which the very goal is the event of truth itself, it is necessary that Actaion does not maintain himself in his original form and not return, for that other moment of truth in which the soul has the purpose of conducting its own, the soul's, boon over into this real life, it is essential that the three brothers *maintain* themselves.

There are innumerable other moments of truth in the soul's life, among them also that moment of truth in which it is the soul's need to conceal itself, veil itself—in obvious contrast to the other need discussed in *The Soul's Logical Life* to encounter itself as naked truth, absolutely unveiled. I mention this fact because some people, e.g., Michael Vannoy Adams, impute to my book the thesis that *all* myths were about the pursuit of absolute Truth, so that they feel the odd need to remind me that there are myths about the veiled, too.

I now want to give at least three more myths as examples for other moments of truth, only three out of the multitude of possible examples, and discuss them only rather sketchily, on top of it. The point for me here is not to do full justice to any of them, but to give some general indication of what is meant by the idea of the soul's "different moments of truth." As examples I have chosen myths in which the soul feels the need to take the guise of a human feminine figure, namely Semele, Danae, Alkmene, that relates to a masculine god, so that we get a real contrast to the two tales of Actaion and the slippery mountain that start out with human masculine figures and have a divine or otherworldly feminine figure as their counterpart.

The myth of Actaion is not about the psychology of men, the myth of Semele not about the psychology of women. "Men" and "women" are not psychological concepts. They belong to biology, anthropology, sociology, etc., whereas psychology is about "the soul." In psychology, images of men and women, the masculine and the feminine, are metaphors or allegories, but what they are metaphors or allegories for is always the soul in one of its guises. Depending entirely on what the particular nature of the truth of itself is that the soul wants to portray, it may need to imagine itself as a masculine or as a feminine (or at times perhaps also as a neutral or hermaphroditic) figure, a figure relating to itself (the soul) in the guise of a figure of the opposite sex (or at times also of the same sex or no sex at all). The sexual form of the figures, rather than being a primary given, is a *function* of the particular notion that is to be portrayed, a function of the specific nature of the respective moments of truth, just as much as are the other specific traits of the same figures and as are the deeds and events in the same myth.

Before I begin, I want to stress that in looking at myths I am concerned solely with the truth displayed in them, that is to say, with notions, concepts. I have no ulterior purpose beyond that of understanding the concept and its internal logic in each case. In this regard it is similar to studying the nature of a triangle in geometry. I do not want anything for myself from it, I do not ask for a practical use or wish to get answers and help for living my life, for better mastering predicaments, for overcoming neurotic conflicts, for improving my self-development or simply for understanding myself better, nor to give some mythic depth to my reality. All such egoic and extraneous concerns I leave behind. Just as the concepts of a triangle or octagon have nothing immediately to do with us and our real lives; but just as a clear comprehension of them differentiates and cultivates the mind, so, too, the study of myths is not about us and our sole purpose in pursuing it should be to learn to comprehend something and thereby to refine the mind. The study of a myth must be free, for interest's sake only, *sine ira et studio*; our study must have everything it needs *within itself*, even its reward. Its purpose is truth, insight, nothing else. "The truth shall make you free," as the Bible says (John 8:32), and "*Magna est vis veritatis et praevalebit*" (Great is the power of truth and it shall prevail), as Jung, probably citing Tertullian,[1] said as early as 1912 (*GW* 7 p. 291, *CW* 7 § 441).

Semele and the moment of the soul's absolute giving itself over to itself in passion

If the soul wants to portray its own need of absolute devotedness and self-abandonment to itself as its other, it chooses a feminine figure. This absolute giving over of herself is tantamount to absolute receptivity and conception. It is *absolute* to the extent that it does not insist on her being preserved in her receiving/conceiving. This need constellates the soul's other in the guise of the begetter, Zeus. If the fathering Zeus approaches Semele in his absolute, pure form as lightning, as totally consuming fire, then this is not to be seen as

---
[1] Tertullian, *Adversus Praxean* 26.

violence and annihilation—at any rate not simply as destructiveness on the part of the begetter, but as the expression of Semele's relentless dedication. The form of her fate to be consumed by the fire and light nature of Zeus reveals her own nature. For it is Semele's own request to see and experience Zeus in his true shape, in his ultimate truth. So this is that moment of the soul's truth when it desires to experience its own truth or rather itself as truth. In a way, this makes it very similar to the Actaion myth, but instead of actively hunting for the (then "naked") truth, pure, virginal truth, which would make it express an interest in *knowing* itself as truth, the Semele myth shows how the soul longs to passively or, rather, passionately totally receive itself as absolute truth or burning fire to the point of being consumed by it, and to thereby also conceive something new. Instead of cognition and seeing (Actaion), total illumination and passionate consumption (Semele). The flash of lightning is not so much something that befalls her from the outside, a mishap, a terrible fate. Rather, her being consumed is actually, or at least just as much, her own consuming of herself in passion, her languishing, her wasting away, desires which crave the consuming flash of lightning for themselves. Semele's sister had the name Thyone, "the rapturous one," and later this name was also given to Semele. This clearly expresses Semele's self-abandonment nature. Absolute passionate giving over of herself and absolutely consuming lightning are the same, though not alike. The flash on the one side reveals the relentlessness and absoluteness of the passionate devotedness on the other side. Naturally so, because myth depicts the soul's self-relation, and therefore we have on both sides the same, the soul in exactly corresponding complementary forms. In real life, two people with their own individual character and history and needs come together; their union is a "synthetic judgment" in the sense given; this is why it may be that they do not fit each other. But the union in myth is the self-display of one notion, the "analytic" unfolding of the soul (one and the same soul) into two, into one out of the multitude of forms of its internal dialectical pairings.

I used the words "languishing," "wasting away." They are not totally correct. The longed for begetter comes to Semele certainly in a violent form, as penetrating, not part of her body, but her total existence. It is *absolute* penetration, indeed permeation. And only as such is it the fundamental dissolution of Semele: absolute passionate fulfillment.

In being consumed or consuming herself, Semele disappears. In the encounter, she cannot hold her place as her other's vis-à-vis. Therefore, she cannot carry her child to full term. She did conceive, but she cannot be mother, cannot be a containing, protecting womb for the child. She is all passionate love for her other, in whom she wants to dissolve, with whom she want to merge, to fuse. So her conception is incomplete, one could even say it is in itself abortive, because she cannot hold the child. Nevertheless, her union was not only for herself, for her own gratification; it was indeed productive, transcending herself. And for this reason I have to correct my assertion that Semele wanted to abandon herself so as to fuse with Zeus. This would not do full justice to her. She actually fuses, not into him, but into the *union* with him: into the fruit of the womb, a Third.

Still, she cannot be mother for her child. The function of mother, of holding uterus, passes over to the begetter, Zeus, and to Zeus not just in general, but probably specifically to him *as* the begetter, for it is precisely the masculine thigh that takes on the function of substitute womb. This, too, is inherent in the logic of Semele's total self-abandonment in passion. She does not persist. In her passion, she sort of dies into the union with her other, and so her own function of pregnant mother is also totally abandoned to, passed over into, that other, Zeus.

Zeus is now begetter, father, sire—*and* mother, carrying the child to term and giving birth to it, at once. The transition of the mother aspect into the father and this counter-natural union of opposites is narratively portrayed as being performed by Hermes. The transition from one ontological or logical realm to another is his domain.

Zeus becomes mother in a sublated, reflected, logically negative sense. He is of course not a natural mother. There is a brokenness, disruption inherent in this motherhood of Zeus.

Who and what is the fruit of this union? (a) Dionysus is *as* masculine god nevertheless of a feminine nature. In him, his mother as the enraptured, enthusiastic one continues to live, confirming once more that Semele indeed fused into the *union* with Zeus, not into Zeus alone. (b) Dionysus is also the god of self-abandonment, both in the sense of enrapturedness, raving, swarming out *and* as maenadic raging, such as tearing living kids of does apart—a violent radicality and destructiveness in which the high voltage of his father as a flash of lightning is reflected. (c) Dionysus is also wine, dissolution, fermenting corruption, dismemberment, in all of which the logical rupture and sublatedness of the womb that carried and gave birth to him express themselves. However, the sublation of nature (e.g., of the natural womb) does not catapult Dionysus out of nature altogether into the sphere of the mind, rationality, the purely noetic, as embodied, e.g., in Apollo or Athene. Rather, in Dionysus we encounter a sublatedness of nature that nevertheless stays completely within nature, a strictly natural, physical, material sublatedness, which comes out very clearly in the symbol of wine. Dionysus is a natural, bodily spirituality: rapture, enthusiasm. If we follow Kerényi, Dionysus expresses the celebration of life's indestructibility, life's power to maintain itself precisely through and despite the cruelty of devouring its own manifestations. The definitely mental Athene was also born directly of Zeus, but she sprang from his head, whereas Dionysus came from his thigh.

Dionysus is, of course, a god in his own right and needs to be viewed as such. But this is not our topic here. Here we have to view him as the outcome of the relation between Semele and Zeus, of the soul's passionately dying into itself in its ultimate form as sheer consuming flash of lightning. How is this kind of an outcome of the consumption and disappearance of the soul in the union with itself as lightning to be understood? Why is there, how can there be, an outcome, a product? In order to understand this I make use of a passage from a letter by Jung, not entirely happily, because Jung is speaking of empirical human life and aspects of the phenomenology of people's behavior, whereas I want to discuss the notion displayed in our myth. Nevertheless, the categories used by Jung in the following passage can give us a clue about what the product of the union of "the soul as pure passionate abandonment" to "itself as pure flash of lightning" is about. Jung says, "It is unfortunately true that when you are wife and mother you can hardly be the hetaira too, just as it is the secret suffering of the hetaira that she is not a mother. There are women who are not meant to bear physical children, but they are those that give rebirth to a man in a spiritual sense, which is a highly important function."[2]

---

[2] C. G. Jung, *Letters 2*, p. 455, to Carol Jeffrey, 18 June 1958.

The soul as Semele does not want to be mother to a child herself. Here the soul wants to abandon itself in passion to the union with itself in order to give rebirth in a spiritual sense to the other of itself, who in this case takes the guise of Zeus. Dionysus is, in the context of *this* discussion, the separate objectification of this rebirth of Zeus through the union with Semele. In real life, we sometimes find that a great artist has a woman who more or less totally dedicates herself to him in order to serve as his muse. The product of this union, too, is an unnatural birth in that the artist as begetter is at once the one who also himself carries the fruit of the womb to term and gives birth to it. But in this case, the product is not the spiritual rebirth of the artist as person, but his work of art.

Danae and the moment of the soul's longing for impregnation by itself

Danae is locked up in a dungeon, in total darkness, in a kind of underworld. The fate that befalls her, her being imprisoned, and the place where she is, tell us what and who she is. Her prison is the reflection of her own nature. The locked up underground room is a totally *containing vessel, receptacle*. Danae *is* thus nothing but womb and mother. She cannot only conceive but also hold the baby, carry it to term; she contains it within her dark dungeon, within the image of the womb, even two or five years beyond its literal birth.

To conceive, the soul must perceive itself as and become totally an underworldly prison. It must completely withdraw from the visible world and everything that ties it to the visible world and be all-invisible womb, receptacle. The ideas of a lover, a relationship, partnership, of desire, lust and the ecstasy of love making have no place here. Conception takes place in the underworld.

The correlate to the soul as Danae who is all-conceiving womb is the rain of gold in which Zeus comes to her. The begetter does not approach her violently, not as intruder-penetrator into her prison or into herself; he does not burst open her prison walls, but seeps or flows into the vessel. Whereas Danae as the conceiving and containing one subsists, Zeus in his guise as seeping rain is, as it were, not existent here as himself, as person and subject, at all; he is reduced to, dissolved into, being no more than the impregnating semen, faceless, anonymous.

However, as gold, it is the mysterious inner substance of mind or spirit, semen in its nature as divine light, the mysterious origin of life.

In comparison with the Zeus of the Semele myth, we could say that the rain of gold is the pacified, contained flash of lightning, first coagulated into solid form (gold), but then this solid form dispersed again or even liquefied into rain.

The notion narratively portrayed in the Danae story is that of the soul that wants to conceive and be pregnant. It is the image of impregnation, conception, and pregnancy *only*. Not of giving birth, not of protecting, nourishing, mothering, raising the born child. Danae, like all mythic figures, is not a person, a human being, but an allegory of one concept. The concept of conception tells us that the correlate to the womb is the semen, not the person whose semen it is. We can recall here that in many ancient cultures the sexual act between man and woman was not thought to be important for procreation. The real father was thought to be a spirit. We still have a trace of this in our culture in the idea of the Virgin Mary being impregnated by the Holy Ghost.

The fruit of this union between Danae and Zeus is Perseus. Just as his mother is underworldly, so he, too, has a relation to the depth of the underworld. The fact that he is able to preserve himself vis-à-vis the Gorgon Medusa reminds us of the solidity of the walls of his mother's prison, whereas in Dionysus we have dismemberment, fermenting corruption, and raving in perfect accordance with the absolute self-abandonment of his mother. The fight with the underworld demon of the Gorgon, unlike those of Hercules, does not have the purpose of simple killing and extinction, but of releasing something precious from out of the depth into life, namely Pegasus, poetry. This might be an effect of the golden rain.

Danae is, like Kore, an underworld figure. However, whereas Kore is in a virginal state and needs to be raped into the underworld, Danae is, as it were, Persephone from the outset, no initiation, no transition from maiden to woman and possible mother (womb) being necessary.

Alkmene and the moment of the soul's establishing itself in pragmatic reality

Semele disappeared in Zeus or in the union with him, Zeus in his union with Danae was reduced to the abstract mysterious-divine origin of life and disappeared in the union with her. In both cases—woman and consuming flash of lightning/woman as solid vessel and seeping rain of gold—the encounter was fundamentally asymmetrical, the one side or the other having a decided preponderance. If Zeus appears to Alkmene in the guise of her husband, Amphytrion, by contrast, she experiences a union between partners of equal standing and weight, a balanced union, in which both persons hold their place firmly in reality. Thus, we have here a true couple. Their union does not occur across a fundamental "species" border between them, both being human.

Alkmene is not a maiden (Kore) and has no underworld connections either, but she is from the outset an accomplished wife in the human social sphere, a *Teleía*.

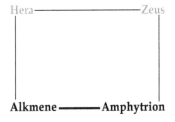

In this sense, her sexual union with her husband is a *hieròs gámos* in the old Greek sense of the word. Nowadays in religious studies this term is used in the new sense introduced by the Neoplatonists (Proclus), as a particular union between gods and as belonging to "mystical tales." But, as Kerényi explains, originally the expression *hieròs gámos* was used for the consummation of a marriage between mortals, especially for the first sexual intercourse if it was performed in accordance with the rites and customs prescribed by Hera. Hera as *Teleía* presides in particular over the transition from the virgin state of a woman to that of the legitimate spouse, accomplished wife (*Teleía*). And the contrast to *hieròs gámos* was *methemerinoì gámoi*, "daily marriages," that is, sexual unions with prostitutes.

In this myth the soul imagines itself as a real empirical human woman in a union with itself as a real empirical human husband. But because this is a *hieròs gámos*, a marriage according to the rules of Hera, who is herself *Teleía*, Alkmene, too, becomes a *Teleía*. In the act performed in the spirit and according to the rules of Hera, the woman precisely *as* human wife *is*—implicitly—herself Hera. And her husband, Amphytrion, *as* human husband participating in the *hieròs gámos*, likewise *is*—implicitly—*ipso facto* Zeus Teleios, the one who brings accomplishment or perfection to his woman (accomplishment as regards the social status of "wife").

So we get a quaternio.[33] On the explicit human empirical level we have the couple Alkmene and Amphytrion, while on the implicit and invisible divine level we have Hera and Zeus. But what is essential here is that the divine level remains invisible, merely implicit; more than that: it is fundamentally sublated, it is not becoming a reality in its own right. Rather, it is here merely the reflection of the inner depth or symbolic meaning of the interhuman relationship in the sense of a *hieròs gámos*. So there is not a real quaternio here. In truth, there are only two realities, Alkmene and Amphytrion, and Hera and Zeus are nothing new and additional to them: they are only the inner divine depth aspect of the two humans themselves if, and for the time that, they perform the rite of a *hieròs gámos*. By performing this rite, they, as it were, put on divine garments. So the gods do not really have an existence of their own here. They are logically completely reflected into the two humans and thus "internal" to them.

In this particular one of the soul's moments of truth that is portrayed in this myth, the soul settles totally into this mundane world, on the empirical human side, in social reality. The fact that "Zeus" appears to Alkmene in the human shape of her own husband reflects that the soul's own other has become humanized, too, and lost its *fundamental* otherness. There is not really a crossing over from this side to the beyond, or vice versa. In fact, a border between two fundamentally different realms, this world and the world yonder, does not come into play here at all. This difference between two realms separated by a fundamental border has been reduced precisely to the ordinary *social* otherness of husband and wife on this side of the border. There is no reaching out for the naked truth to be found in the wilderness, or for the princess with the golden apples on the glass mountain, and no languishing for being visited by the absolutely consuming flash of lightning or for the

---

[3] But note the difference to the quaternios that Jung works with, where the transcendent (internal, unconscious, archetypal) other of a person is counter-sexual (e.g., the Adept and his Anima, the Soror and her Animus).

divine rain of gold to be received/conceived by a dark underworldly vessel, either. The soul, in this one of its moments of truth, contents itself with being fully human and establishing itself in positive reality. An initiation or a real encounter of the soul with itself as its own other or an adventurous advance on the part of the soul to its own hard-to-reach land has no place here.

In terms of cultural history, we might say that the stage of mythic-ritualistic existence has here been left and the sphere of religion has been entered, religion in which the gods are no longer epiphanies, experienced realities in nature (so to speak *universalia in re*), living vis-à-vis, but *have become mental*, have receded into the human mind and thus now have only a sublated *symbolic* existence in one's faith or pious attitude, as conceptions in the human imagination (so to speak *universalia in mente*) and as contents of one's *interpretation* of real life. As the intended objects of one's worshiping upward looking, they affirm man's one-sided stationing himself in *this* world and merely "dreaming" of the other. In the present case, Hera and Zeus are merely the formulation of the fact that the real social phenomenon of a marriage as real by and in itself and as self-sufficient is experienced as having (or is assigned) its own *internal* depth and higher (religious) meaning. The situation is of course not yet a modern, depth-psychological one, where the gods would be imagined as images in ourselves, in our own unconscious. Rather, the gods and religious meaning are here social factors, personified expressions of the values and rules of a social community (in our case values and rules concerning marriage) *and* at the same time the personification of the absolute authority that authorizes those values. But abstract-formally (structurally) there is already a certain similarity to the modern situation in that a real beyond such as expressed in the top of the glass mountain has already been written off, and in that gods are only ideas or images in the human mind.

However, with the *hieròs gámos* the meaning of the Alkmene story is not exhausted. There is a totally other aspect that complicates matters. In his union with Hera, Zeus is the brother-husband. As such he or Amphytrion would make Alkmene-Hera into the *Teleía*, but he would not father a child. Zeus fathers only when he is not brother-husband, but when he is *the wider, mysterious origin of life* (that appeared to Danae as the rain of gold and to Semele as the flash of lightning). The normal sexual act between humans as *hieròs gámos* is not in itself procreative. It can only become procreative if in addition the mysterious and spiritual origin of life comes into play, too. The latter has nothing to do "archetypally" with the ordinary human sexual act, but is something independent stemming from an entirely different "ontological" or "archetypal" realm, which may accompany it or not. It is a special characteristic of Greek mythology that the one God Zeus embodies these two almost opposite functions.

So we do not have a simple marriage quaternio. It is complicated because Zeus appears here in two different functions, the one being his appearing as part of the quaternio, the other his intruding into it. In the first sense, he is simply Hera's brother-husband and as such the inner depth aspect of Amphytrion as the normal husband that Amphytrion is. Up to this point, everything is *comme il faut*. In every legitimate sexual union, there are these two levels, the level of the empirical human and the empirical events' inner meaning level of the divine couple. But here Zeus is *also* and in addition present as the flashing shine of the mystery of the mysterious origin of life, something comparable to the Holy Ghost. However, the point in this one of the soul's moments of truth is again that the spiritual fathering force completely *conceals* itself in the guise of the normal, the ordinary, of the empirically real and familiar. It does not become visible and explicit; in fact, it remains completely unnoticed. The mysterious spiritual or divine origin of life is hidden and occluded in the factual consummation of the marriage. The soul here does not want to confront itself with a direct epiphany or revelation of Zeus as the begetter, as it occurred with Semele or Danae, or, for that matter, with the Virgin Mary (the Annunciation).

Only after the fact, when there is a discrepancy between the experiences of Alkmene and of Amphytrion, is the involvement of Zeus as an Other *inferred*. In this sense, the soul side in its fundamental otherness does become present in this story, after all; however, only as a conjecture, not as a revelation. As an inference, as a conjecture, the presence of Zeus is just an *idea* in the human mind. Realistically speaking this conjecture boils down to the observation that Alkmene has become pregnant. In the present myth, this fact is *explained* religiously as the mysterious origin of life (and not just the human husband) having been with Alkmene, whereas for us today the just-as-unpredictable diagnosis of a state of pregnancy does not need and does not receive a religious interpretation. We leave it unexplained and without religious depth as a merely biological chance event, an accidental happening in the sphere of positivity with no *meaning* whatsoever. So even with respect to Zeus as the mysterious origin of life we have to realize that in this particular constellation the religious stance (in contrast to the ritualistic or initiatory one) prevails and that the soul here too has settled on the human side and allows for the reality of the presence of the divine only via speculation after the fact, not as immediate initiatory experience.

Any child coming out of a *hieròs gámos* is *ipso facto* a Herakles, a glory of Hera. But Hera is also jealous of this child, because she knows that the father cannot be her brother-husband or that Zeus did not confine himself to being her brother-husband and in this sense escaped her, was unfaithful to her.

Herakles as the fruit of this union belongs completely to the empirical world. His task is to establish firmly and stabilize the human stance in this, the empirical world, in social reality, and protect it from the onrush of the soul's other side, which now is put down as monstrous. It is for this reason that he must fight and eliminate the underworld monsters, one after another—not to win a boon from them, but to more securely shut the door to the other side altogether. As fully rooted in the human social sphere, he has to perform *labors*. And similarly, he has to be the great *sufferer*, much like Jesus Christ (God having become man on this earth), without his suffering having in any way the nature of an *initiation* (as for example with Dionysus). It is just plain suffering, plain pain. But the other side of this this-worldliness of his is that in the end, in his afterlife, he is received into Olympus[4] and marries Hebe, the younger version of Hera. This duality of spheres corresponds of course to the duality of the levels in the marriage quaternio and to the fact that the soul in this particular one of its moments of truth has entered the "religious" stage and imagines itself accordingly.

Herakles could not have been the product of the union between

---

[4] The many parallels between Herakles and Christ (Christ as God having become fully man, Christ as victor over the underworld, Christ's resurrection) were noticed and appreciated by the early Church.

Semele and the flash of lightning, nor between Danae and the rain of gold. Conversely, a Perseus or a Dionysus could not possibly have been the offspring of Alkmene's union with Zeus as Amphytrion. In myth, the parents and the form of union on the one hand and their child and its characteristics on the other mutually explain each other. They are tautegorical. Now, Herakles is, *within* mythology, that figure that actively closes the mythological-ritualistic mode of being-in-the-world and thereby prepares the ground for that new stance that is characterized by religion and philosophy, metaphysics.

CHAPTER THREE

The Historicity of Myth

WOLFGANG GIEGERICH

With respect to his psychological typology C. G. Jung warned against superficially picking up his typological terminology ("extraverted thinking type," e.g.) "since," as he said, "this serves no other purpose than the totally useless desire to stick on labels" (*CW* 6, p. xv). Although Jung's typology makes do with eight possible classes, whereas mythology offers innumerable figures and stories, it is also possible to stick myths on people or on life events. For every behavior, every life situation, most dream images, you can surely find some suitable myth. But to look for such correspondences would be not much different from "the totally useless desire" "to stick labels on" phenomena, for it would be no more than a mechanical pairing of two sets of items according to external similarities, a task known from certain card games for very young children. In Molière's *Le bourgeois gentilhomme*, the newly-rich, vain, but ignorant and naive Monsieur Jourdain learns for the first time that he is speaking "prose," which makes him stalk around as if with this new-found label from classical rhetoric and stylistics his speech had become ennobled and classical, too. But his talking is of course exactly the same as before. Similarly, our personalities, predicaments, conflicts stay just as ordinary and human, all-too-human, when we stick mythic or divine labels on them as when we do not. Myths, I believe, should not be used to ennoble what in itself is not mythic at all.

For we have to take into account the gulf that separates us and our life from myth. We and "myth" do not live in the same world. Our relation to myth is inevitably archaeological: during the last two centuries myth had to be excavated, unearthed (cf. the title of an anthology by Karl Kerényi, *Die Eröffnung des Zugangs zum Mythos* [*The Opening up of the Access to Myth*]), as fossilized relics of the past, after having been dead and buried for ages, covered by layers and layers of other stages of cultural and psychological development. This is what I want to discuss or rather merely touch on in the following. The gulf (which actually is a plural of sequential gulfs) can be seen above all from three perspectives, from that of:

- the locus of knowledge,
- the form (constitution) of time and world (mundus), *and*
- the relation of separation and union *or* of identity and difference,

of which for time reasons I will discuss today only the first.

What enables myths to be immediately applied to modern life situations is, paradoxically, that the concept of myth has been fundamentally reduced, abstracted to mean a *narrative*. As a narrative, myth is (logically) dead. By being abstracted from its time (like a medieval altarpiece in a modern museum, removed from its original context in the living piety of its age), it has become universalized and forfeited its nature as living myth, and thus as *myth* in the first place. For it is indispensable to the notion of myth to mean living myth; how else if not as living myth could it encompass the depth of existence as such and express its meaning (which is what myth is expected to do)? Myth therefore has to be comprehended as the unity of myth in the sense of a narrative *and* of the whole status of consciousness or mode of being-in-the-world of the specific age that gave birth to myths and whose self-expression of its inner logic the mythic tales used to be; in other words, it has to be comprehended as the unity of mythic narrative *and* the mythological-ritualistic mode of being-in-the-world, the unity of (mythological) semantics and (mythological) syntax.[1]

Jung bypassed this insight because he resorted, with a circular argument, to the idea of universal psychological factors ("archetypes-in-themselves") of which the known myths are only temporary and culture-specific expressions. It does not matter here whether archetypes are conceived as biological or metaphysical, as innate or as acquired and inherited, as a residue of collective experience or whatever—in any case Jung's idea of archetypes metaphysically substantiates the psyche as a *Hinterwelt*, a positive-factual reality behind reality, and solidifies the belief that one could go *behind* the phenomena (behind the myths, etc.) to positively existing noumenal factors that *produced* the phenomena.[2] With this belief in a literal universal, in an anthropological constant, in a positivized, allegedly "empirical" noumenal, as the hidden source of mythology, one gets two advantages. If accepted, it indeed legitimizes the belief that *mutatis mutandis* the ancient myths are, just like that, still capable of expressing the psychological depth of our modern life, and secondly, it allows one to reduce the admitted historical change to irrelevance, because the positivized noumenal, i.e., the archetypes, invalidates any phenomenal cultural rupture by providing a bypass via the atemporal universal. The only problem with this way of thinking, this bypass operation, is that this legitimizing assumption is itself not legitimate: for we are not permitted to invent a positively existing psyche *behind* psychological phenomenology. There *is* no such thing as a soul that produces psychological phenomena. The phenomena have nothing behind them. They have everything they need within themselves, even their own origin, their author or subject. "The soul" in my parlance thus does not refer to something real outside of, distinct from, and

---

[1] Just as one should not abstract the narrative form out of this unity of narrative and mode of being-in-the-world, one should of course just as much avoid the converse abstraction. One should not abstract "the mythological mode of being-in-the-world" from this unity, e.g., in the form of the abstract idea of a universal, free-floating, anthropological factor, of the mere *syntax* (and thus eternal potential) of mythic thinking as an ahistorical (and as such inescapable) underlying deep structure of the mind. Myth is concrete, embodied in actual tales. It is the unity of syntax and semantics.

[2] Jung's trick was to disguise his *metaphysical* move before himself and us by claiming that his archetypes, "the unconscious," the soul, etc., were just *empirical facts*. So it seemed to him that it was not his, but empirical reality's fault if he discovered a *Hinterwelt* behind the phenomenal world.

in addition to psychological phenomenology, but is no more than a still mythologizing, personifying, *façon de parler*, an expression for the inner *soul quality*, *depth*, and *internal infinity*, of the phenomena themselves, as well as for their internal "teleology." "The soul" is thus, contrary to appearances, an "adjective" or "adverb," not a noun. The noun character is only rhetorical, not substantial. But if there is nothing, especially not anything atemporal, behind historical phenomenology, then the historical differences between the phenomena make a real, decisive difference: their logical form and the status of consciousness in which they exist and that determines what they psychologically *are*. This is why we have to study the gulf I spoke of.

The historical gulf from the point of view of the locus of knowledge

I speak in this paper of a mythological-ritualistic stage in contradistinction to later stages as if the former were one unitary stage and did not itself have to be differentiated within itself into several different phases. But for our purposes here I do not want to complicate matters, so I treat it as one more-or-less homogeneous whole. (Another problem that I ignore here is whether "myth" and "mythological" are really the most adequate terms: whether what they refer to is the most characteristic and authentic phenomenon to designate this stage. Ritual, e.g., might be more significant.)

I begin my rather impressionistic description with a quote from a book on the dream-time narrations of the Australian aborigines. "Unlike what we are used to from our fairy tales, whose narration starts with one event, continues with the next and leads to an end, the dream-time stories of the [Australian] aborigines do neither have a beginning nor an end. Like an unending band they flow along, merge into each other, intertwine and disentangle again, break up abruptly, only to reappear, like a subterranean watercourse, at another place."[3]

What does that tell us? A consciousness that does not feel the need or have the strength to clearly demarcate beginning and end, thereby creating separate stories, but for which *all* images and narrative events *together*

---

[3] Heiner Uber, "Bahlu, der Mond und Yurlunggur, die Regenbogenschlange: Ein Vorwort," Piet Bogner, *Traumzeit-Erzählungen der Aborigines*, (Munich: Mosaik Verlag, 1999), p. 8.

THE HISTORICITY OF MYTH

represent a living, ever-changing interconnected whole from which they cannot be separated into individual units, is, as it were, floating in an infinite ocean. Or we could say it lives on the level of a rhizome. All the dream-time narratives together make up ONE immense narrative. In the ocean you may have different currents, different pockets of warmer or colder water, but it is all one inseparable body of water. Just as you cannot look at all the details of a large painting at once, so here, too, you can speak about only one detail of the ONE narrative at a time, but just as you can wander through all the depicted details of the painting in different ways, starting here or there, jumping from one place to another, etc., so here too. You focus always on one partial sequence of events at a time, but when you focus on it, you get the whole rhizome in the bargain. If you raise the Midgard Serpent above ground in one place, you have touched the whole Midgard Serpent. The factual beginning and end of narrations are here brought about only by extraneous circumstances: you get tired, nightfall or a thunderstorm or practical necessities disrupt your narration, but beginning and end have not been reflected or integrated *into the stories themselves* as part of their form and thus are not the tales' own self-closure.

This is probably an extreme expression of the mythic mode of being-in-the-world. But precisely because it is extreme it highlights all the better an essential feature of that status of consciousness. When, by contrast, in Greece Homer or Hesiod tell mythic tales in their epics, the tales not only have their clear beginning and end, but the authors freely dispose of the individual tales, which are therefore reduced to (sublated) moments in a larger poetic scheme. This is most obvious in Hesiod, who in his *Theogony* tries to organize the many traditional mythic tales in a systematic order according to a temporal *ordering principle*. Here each tale not only has its own closure, but the very topic of "*the* beginning" (of all) is on top of it made into the literal beginning of the whole work and thought (just as the ancient editors who put together the Old Testament set the creation story at the beginning of the Bible). In a time of living myth this would not make sense at all, since each significant Now, each Now of a performed ritual, was *ipso facto* a moment of the creation of the world and had "the beginning" within itself, not in a historical past prior to itself or in another, preceding tale. Here consciousness obviously is no longer completely floating in the infinite ocean of mythic images, but has a stance vis-à-vis the images and even an overview of them. Myth has been *ipso facto* reduced to "literature." We now have determinate tales. In both Homer and Hesiod consciousness has, in different ways, stepped out of the mythic mode of being-in-the-world and independently established itself. Homer and Hesiod transmit many mythic tales, but they are no longer true myths in the sense of the unity of narrative and mythic status of consciousness. Myth proper is already dead, antiques.

With the aborigines, it was not really the narrator who tells a tale. Rather, the narrator dives into the ocean of dream-time at a particular place and allows the dream or myth to surface through him. The tale, as it were, told itself, and it could do so because the so-called narrator had immersed himself in the infinite medium of mythic truth, allowing himself to be carried by its waves and being permeated by them. Just like the aborigine is completely tuned in to his environment and the climate and the seasons, conceiving of himself as an integral element of this whole of nature rather than as a subject vis-à-vis nature, a subject that approaches the world with ignorance and questions that demand *explanations*, so, when telling tales, he is completely contained in the dream-time and, without will of his own, determined by its internal life. Homer and Hesiod, by contrast, are active narrators, even if they are certainly not yet subjects in the post-medieval sense. The clear separation between them as narrators and the stories they tell finds an independent expression in Greece in the idea of the muses as the actual tellers of the tales. The poets do not speak as subjects on their own responsibility, but they are no longer totally immersed in the ocean of mythic knowledge either, the muses *mediating* between them and their stories, i.e., *separating* the poets from, and at once connecting them with, what is to be told.

I start again with another example. Scholars have pointed out that in inscriptions on statues in early Greek times the statue is immediately identified with the person represented. The text on such a statue might, e.g., be: "I am Chares, the ruler of Teichiussa." Athens, however, was an exception. Here the inscription would read: "I am the depiction, the tomb, the monument, of such and such."[4] The geographical difference (Athens versus other places) expresses a temporal one between later

---

[4] See Bruno Snell, *Die Entdeckung des Geistes* (Göttingen: Vandenhoeck & Ruprecht, 1975), p. 101, and my discussion in *Die Atombombe als seelische Wirklichkeit*, Zürich 1988, pp. 186ff. and *Drachenkampf oder Initiation ins Nuklearzeitalter*, Zürich 1989, p. 66.

THE HISTORICITY OF MYTH

and earlier stages in the development of consciousness, Athens or Attica being ahead of its time. What does it tell us that the statue in the earlier situation categorically declares, "*I am* Chares, the ruler ..."? The statue here is not a representation of the absent ruler, it *is* immediately his real presence. But how can it be his presence, his reality? Because it is his *image*. The nature of the image in that (mythic) stage is that it has, to use a poor expression, an absolute suggestive power. The image is here *a priori* true because it is image. It is not the other way around; the fact that it correctly depicts some reality outside of itself is not what makes it true. The image as image has everything it needs within itself. Looking at it, consciousness is *a priori* captivated by it, prepossessed, seduced into imagining or imaging it as unquestionable truth. There is no consciousness here that could hold itself as a separate existence vis-à-vis the image and clearly distinguish itself from it. Rather, it is absorbed into its sphere, floating in it as in an ocean of truth. ("The ocean" does not have to refer to the inseparable whole of the ONE image as which the Australian dream-time exists; here a single individual image is an "ocean" unto itself.) As floating in it, consciousness does not have the image before itself as its content or its object of vision, but is conversely contained by it on all sides. It is a situation of absolute inness in the image.

This is also, by the way, why the statue can truly say, "I am the *ruler*...," because *as* an image it rules over consciousness as the latter's truth. The image does not need any justification, legitimization, proof, and it *is* immediately the *ruler*, not because it refers to Chares and his positive-factual political and military power, but rather the other way around: because the literal Chares-in-the-flesh also receives *his* authority as ruler from the mythic image of ruler, which is what gives him his charisma, his mystical *Königsheil*. Even his literal presence is his presence *as image, as the image of ruler*. The image does not only have its truth within itself, but it also has within itself him, to whom it "refers" (as we have to say from the newer point of view). He, too, is absorbed into its aura. Vestiges of this status of consciousness can be found even today, e.g., in the experience of Roman Catholic believers with relics, pictures of saints and Black Madonnas. The splinter of the cross *is* the true splinter of the cross owing to its immediately evoking the image of the wooden cross, the image that has its truth within itself and is thus not in need of any verification; its truth is absolutely immune to the fact that all the splinters of the cross in the world joined together would make several large crosses. External arguments are irrelevant, they are simply a misunderstanding of the nature of the mythic image.

If in Athens the statue refers to itself as a *representation* of Chares, then consciousness and image part ways, as do image and what must now be called referent. Consciousness has the image as a clearly demarcated object before itself, and the image has what it represents outside of itself as a now positively existing reality that in turn receives its reality and authority from its positive existence, not from the image. And the image now receives its truth from its likeness to that which it represents. Now, and only now, can the image be true *or* false and thus questionable. The new status of consciousness has dissolved the immediacy that characterized the mythic mode of being-in-the-world. At least potentially, there is a fourth separation that may take place along with this making the image explicit *as* image, i.e., *as* the mediating third between the viewer and the reality referred to. The fourth separation—in addition to the splits between consciousness and image, image and referent, true and false—is the difference between different individuals who may each have their own view of a given image. By contrast, in the mythic stage, the image was (not a collective, but) a *communal* truth, inasmuch as it had, as mythic image, *a priori* absorbed into itself as unquestionable truth all the members of the community.

A curious small example from a much later age for the fact that the mythically perceived image has its truth within itself is the following. In the coastal areas of Italy, Spain, Portugal, and France, St. Erasmus was venerated as a patron of sailors. His attribute was a ship's windlass with the anchor rope wrapped around it. When his picture came to inland areas, this attribute was interpreted as his intestines having been pulled out of his body with a torture instrument during his martyrdom, and so in those inland areas he became not only a patron of wood turners, but also a helper against abdominal pains. The fact that this is, historically and factually speaking, due to a misinterpretation in no way discredits its religious truth. The mythic image is not the literal picture in its positivity, but what is actually *seen* in it or makes its presence felt. The "same" attribute of the saint *was* indeed in coastal areas a windlass with ropes, while in the inland areas it was just as truly his intestines. Because the image has everything it needs within itself, not even the material substrate of the image, i.e., the positive *picture*, can testify against the truth of the image, quite apart from what image people in former times or other areas might have seen in the same picture.

I started out with the form of narratives in the dream-time of Australian aborigines and continued with the early statues in most areas of Greece expressly declaring themselves *to be* what for us and for the early Athenians they only *represent*. Both are examples of the reality of the image. Now we have to see that in the mythological-ritualistic mode of being-in-the-world not only did certain narratives or statues open up the image reality, but inness in image was the general character of existence. Just as the real or literal Chares, too, is contained in the image, in the statue of him, and is not a separate positive reality vis-à-vis it, because the difference between image and referent does not exist here, so reality as a whole, nature, the world, was not a positivity. The IMAGE, which now does not mean *particular* image, but the general logical status of image, has everything, all reality, within itself. Everything, every event is primarily *image*, imaginal, *phainomenal* and as such at least potentially epiphanic. Everything is enwrapped in mythic garments and not hard-core fact. This means that consciousness lives on the level of *immediate* experience. The fact that all the separations that I mentioned have not yet happened in this situation means that consciousness itself is immersed and floating in its own experiences, without distance to it. Because of the prevailing immediacy, man experiences himself primarily as a thread woven into the fabric of nature, as contained in the course of events uninterruptedly interacting, without his having any arbitrary volition of his own (Heino Gehrts).

But my speaking of "experiences" is already misplaced. The point is precisely that in this stage there is no consciousness in man that would *experience* what happens out there. Rather, man has his "consciousness" and his "soul" and his "insights" in what is, in and as the events themselves, in and as nature, in and as reality, in and as the world. We could say he has his consciousness not in himself but "out there," if it were not for the fact that strictly speaking there is no "out there" for him at this stage inasmuch as he is himself a part of and woven into the "out there." Myth thus is not *fabula*, not a genre of oral literature; myth does not have its locus in human consciousness at all, as human knowing, thinking, feeling. Man has not yet become psychological man. There is no room for belief or faith in what the myths talk about. Myth *is* immediately the truth of nature and life, it is nature's knowing. Later, truth would be comprehended as the correspondence of intellect and reality. But here this concept is totally out of place, because here there is no human intellect standing vis-à-vis reality. Myth is not a theory *about* the world or life; there are no hypotheses, no belief systems here. No, truth, which expresses itself in myth, is here a *subsisting reality*. In the narratives it is the voice of nature itself speaking, similar to birds singing. Just as we can hear the songs of birds, some people can hear the voice of nature.

So man's whole spiritual and intellectual life and his truths and insights had their place in objectivity, not subjectivity, in:

- *Natural events*, earthquakes, the flight of birds, the flash of lightning, the intestines of animals. They were, like omens, immediate loci of knowledge.
- *Significant objects* such as a man's spear or sword or staff, a woman's basket, amulets, a person's tree of life, the banner of a military unit, etc. They were their soul. The soul was not in the person or in the community of people, it was located in particular precious things, in the sacred victims for sacrificial killings, in the sacred personages as the king or Pharaoh, totally invested there, submerged and enclosed in them. But it was their soul because consciousness was immediately connected with the objective world in a primordial identity, rather than being something in its own right vis-à-vis the world.
- Another most significant locus of man's spiritual life was his own *ritual acts*, above all his sacrificial killings. It is essential to realize that one did not have any thoughts accompanying these rituals, nor any feelings or emotions. The action just happened, was performed and as such it was self-sufficient: *it* had as an objective action everything it needed within itself, even its rationality and feeling-value. It *was* truth, *was* meaning and intellectual operation, *was* important. Human thinking, feeling, imagining were left entirely to the objective ritual acts themselves, as inherent

in them. Those acts did not need our subjective thoughts or appreciation on top of it. The moment there is a need to think something about the ritual, to *understand* it or to subjectively have pious feelings regarding it while it is performed, the ritualistic mode of being-in-the-world has been left.

In a certain passage Hegel points, among other things, to the idea of the *signatura rerum* in medieval philosophy and similarly to the instinct of animals that, e.g., leads them to the proper herbs that heal them when they are sick. Then he states that natural man, too, sees into the heart of things and continues, "The same relation is found in sleep, in somnambulism [...]. Reasonable consciousness [*Das vernünftige Bewußtsein*] has here become silent and instead the inner sense has awakened, of which one can say that one's knowing is much more in the identity with the world, with the surrounding things, than in one's being awake. [...] This is why people think this condition is something higher than the sane one. Thus it can be that one has a presentiment of things that happen one thousand hours away. Among savage peoples one finds such a knowing, such a divining to a much higher degree than among the educated ones."[5]

The point for us is that the knowing is here *in the identity with the world, with the surrounding things,* rather than in the waking mind itself (a mind having the world vis-à-vis itself). Whereas in the modern situation such special states of consciousness as somnambulism or sleep are indeed due to the fact that "reasonable consciousness" has become silent, in the mythological-ritualistic status of consciousness that I am concerned with, this consciousness as man's own possession had not yet or only partially awakened, the "natural unity of the intellectual [*Geistigen*] and the natural" (Hegel) or the sympathetic world relation not yet having been dissolved.

Lévy-Bruhl's intuition about a "prelogical mentality" and a "*participation mystique*" was basically right, and his critics, such as Paul Radin and, in other ways, Claude Lévi-Strauss, simply did not understand that such assessments as "prelogical" refer to the psycho-logic of the objective mind, of the culture, i.e., the psycho-logic inherent in myth, in the shamanistic or the ritualistic mode of life, in

---

[5] G. W. F. Hegel, *Vorlesungen über die Philosophie der Religion I*, Theorie Werkausgabe vol.16, pp. 269f., my transl.

magic and divination practices, in primitive art, etc., rather than to the *personalistic* psychology of *people*. The thesis is, of course, not that primitives as people were devoid of reason and governed solely by emotions and impulses. The claim of a move "From Mythos to Logos" is about a shift within the logical constitution of the mind. It is an inner-logical, mind-internal *form* distinction, rather than a hypothesis about a literal, material absence of *logos* in early times and a (then absolutely mysterious) first emergence of *logos* later.

If you want to understand questions of the kind that we are dealing with here, you must not focus personalistically on people and what *they* as individuals say and feel, nor on their positivistically perceived behavior. The question is, what do the rituals that they perform, the myths that they have, say: what is *their* logic? And what does the fact say that these people *have the need* in the first place *to perform* such rituals and *to have* such myths? Our standpoint has to be the *psychological* one, i.e., the standpoint of the level of myth and ritual, of the "objective psyche" (Jung), the "objective mind," and the "absolute mind" (Hegel). Psychologically (not personalistically) it is true what Jung said about primitive man: "He is like a child, only half born, still enclosed in his own psyche as in a dream, in *the* world *as it really is*, not yet distorted by the difficulties of understanding that beset a dawning intelligence" (*CW* 8 § 682).[6] On the personalistic level, Lévy-Bruhl's and Jung's critics of course had to discover that primitives are not children, not just dreaming, but capable of arguing rationally and that they do try to *explain* certain aspects of reality, too. This discovery is true, but not to the point. The point is that primitive man's *essential knowledge* is not *derived from* rational argumentation and from empirical observation, but from immediate "identity with the world," from the self-evidence and suggestive power of the image, from epiphanic and visionary experience, from the immersion into "dream-time." We have to see through the naiveté that takes statements like "He is like a child" personalistically and wants to stay ignorant of the "psychological difference."

---

[6] N.B.: The italicized words are not for emphasis, but mark text that has been left out in the English translation and has been added by me according to the German original.

THE HISTORICITY OF MYTH

Because the locus of this knowing is *in* the identity with the world, it does not really have the character of a *knowing proper* (a subjective act), but rather of *a natural event*. Knowing is here, as it were, something "ontological," not something logical, mental, or noetic, truth having, as we said, the character of a subsisting entity. If we want to hold on to the view that there is a consciousness here, it is an "objective" implicit consciousness, a consciousness on the level of the "fish eyes" discussed by Jung and located in nature, a consciousness that, as it were, stares at you, not, the other way around, one that beholds or observes its contents lying before itself: it is not man's own subjective consciousness *about* nature.

This has consequences for the type of learning that belongs to this stage. I mention three aspects:

(a) With respect to the *essential knowledge*: Instead of teaching and indoctrination, you have on this stage *initiation*, i.e., one's individual total immersion into "the dream-time" or its equivalent. The highest truths had to be experienced immediately, by you yourself, as your own visions, through your own ordeal, etc. Initiation is that process by which the (on this level generally existing) implicit condition of floating in the ocean of truth was individually made explicit and personally actualized through relentless exposure to it (symbolic death) and thereby reaffirmed for the whole tribe.

(b) With respect to *practical knowledge*: In many traditional African societies today it is still considered highly improper for children who are watching their fathers making tools to ask them questions about how they are doing it and why in that particular way. Children are supposed to observe silently: learning *through unconscious osmosis and subconscious imitation*, not through acquiring abstract conceptual knowledge (theory). The know-how is in one's hands, one's body, and "in" the material (the wood or what) to be worked on, not in the thinking mind.

(c) Again with respect to *essential knowledge*: The tribe's traditional tales, gnomes, lays, verses, stereotyped ritual formulas had to be *memorized*. Memorized without explanation, interpretation, or explicit intellectual understanding. You did not have to, were not supposed to, understand conceptually what was said and meant, or rather: this possibility simply did not exist. Instead, you had to be able to repeat it correctly, preserving exactly every word of the age-old tradition. This was so because the understanding was the *text's* understanding itself, its self-sufficient truth, which resided in the correct wording and the event of the correct voicing of the words, not in the receiving mind. You had to know the essential knowledge *by heart*, instead of having a knowledge *about* it.

Because of man's identity with the world, with the surrounding things, with the words spoken and the ritual acts performed, rituals and sacraments could indeed "work." But of course they did not work in our modern subjective sense, providing personal high feelings and the like. The effect, too, was an objective one, the ritual having even its effect self-sufficiently and "objectively" within itself, and man participated in this beneficial effect through his being immediately connected with, or tuned into, the objective logic invested in the ritual through that "objective" identity, through a kind of unsevered umbilical cord.

* * *

But then there was a time both in ancient Greece and in ancient Israel—I restrict myself here to these two places most important for Western culture—a time when this identity was dissolved and an abstraction from this immediacy took place. In Greece the mind pulled away from immediate, concrete, sensual-imaginal, experience and became conscious of itself in contradistinction to the environment, thereby establishing itself as consciousness. This was the initial awakening of the "reasonable consciousness" from its previous slumber, the radical departure from what Hegel calls the "inner sense," and thus the move "from mythos to logos" (and thus to philosophical, metaphysical man). The locus of knowledge was now the mind, later consciousness, and knowledge was knowledge *about* the world that was now indeed vis-à-vis the mind. In this new mode of being-in-the-world, what consciousness had to begin with was not knowledge, but only *ideas* about the world (*Vorstellungen*), assumptions, hypo-theses (imputations), that could be true or false, i.e., were on principle questionable, and therefore required a *logon didonai*, a rational accounting for and a verification—be it rational or empirical. All of a sudden consciousness had become itself responsible for what it thought

THE HISTORICITY OF MYTH

to be true. It had to *think*. Truth thus resided in the ideas (propositions) of consciousness, *if* they corresponded to reality. And only in that case did the ideas become knowledge.

Above, we already looked at examples of the emergence from an identity with the world in other areas, the example of the form of narratives, which changed from veritable myth to the poetic works of Homer and Hesiod, and the example of the status of sculptures, where we noted the shift from "I am Chares" to "I am the image of …" in Attica. Another plastic illustration of the move from the former immediacy into abstraction is Anaximander's inventing and creating a map of the earth. The possibility of a map requires a mind that has logically fundamentally distanced itself from, and positioned itself high above, the world and thus reduced the earth to a sublated moment or content of its consciousness, a small-scale and streamlined *model* of the world. The mind must have had the power to abstract from all real, minute details and immediate sensual-imaginal impressions to give us only the general structure or outline, and along with it an overview of the whole. This entails also that the mind had risen to the *abstract notion* of the earth; it had evaporated and condensed the sensual manifold of reality into a *conceptual* idea of it, a change that ultimately culminates in the mind's arriving at the utterly abstract concept of Being, the basic concept of all metaphysics. It also entails that the real world vis-à-vis consciousness is, as sensually visible and accessible, no longer immediately identical with the mythic-imaginal ("archetypal") conception of the world[7]; rather, it has in principle been reduced to an empirical-factual world (although in practice,

---

[7] In mythological times, any village and any place where a ritual was performed (*regardless* of its particular empirical-physical appearance) was imaginally *ipso facto* the center of the world, and in this center rose the world tree or the step mountain that towers into heaven, the Indian *Meru*, the glass mountain of the fairy tales. And at the concrete horizon from this place there flowed, for mythic knowing, the primordial river, the ocean, again regardless of the literal geographic conditions at those places where from the present viewpoint the horizon was. Independent of where man at the mythological-ritualistic stage of consciousness was at a given time, he was essentially always in the center. The mythic image of the world as heaven-connected center and, at the distance of the horizon, as surrounded by an ocean accompanied man wherever he went and established himself. This mythic, i.e., logically negative knowledge of the world was superimposed over the physical (positive) appearance of the world and was not really contradicted by the factual knowledge that there were other villages that were just as much the center of the world for *their* inhabitants and that beyond the present horizon the world continued despite the imaginal ocean that actually marked the absolute border of the world, the border between being and non-being.

especially in the early times of this new mode, it was still enwrapped in many mythic garments, which could in fact be stripped off only in the course of time).

Above I stated that earlier man had experienced himself as a thread woven into the fabric of nature. The mind's newly gained power to abstract from the sensual-imaginal reality of nature presupposed that it, the mind (not people!), had logically, as mind, torn itself loose, pulled itself out, of this fabric so as to gain a posture vis-à-vis it. A radical negation of that primary immersion of the mind in the natural world, that had found its adequate expression in myth, must have taken place: a divorce of its sympathetic, "symbiotic" unity with nature. And in the will and strength to actually perform this divorce, thereby cutting, as it were, into its own flesh, the mind came into its own. The locus of truth or knowing changed "from nature to mind."

Part of this whole new development is the invention of the idea and feeling of "guilt," which made the tragic sense of life possible and necessary. Guilt is a concept that did not have any place in the mythological status of consciousness. How could it have, if man there was in an identity with the world? There could be mistakes, wrong moves, defilement, but not guilt in a moral sense. Likewise, the concept of punishment is incompatible with the mythological mode of being-in-the-world. What looks like punishment to us, was actually initiations into the truth of the person's deed, the ultimate consequence of the course of events begun with that deed with which the doer stepped outside the protected human sphere and transgressed into the realm of mysteries, the numinous, the tremendum.

"Guilt" here must not be taken at face value. It has nothing to do with immoral deeds, with a fault. It is a strictly psychological phenomenon. The emergence of the idea and experience of guilt simply reflects the logical act of the mind's divorce of its symbiotic unity with nature, through which it came into its own, became explicit mind, *logos*. The phenomenon of "guilt" is thus nothing but the *form* in which the new posture vis-à-vis nature retains within itself an (implicit, *ansichseiend*) awareness of its *contra naturam* origin and thus of its own authentic nature as mind. "Guilt (as such)" or (in Kantian language) "pure guilt" is the birthmark of the mind.

THE HISTORICITY OF MYTH

It hardly needs mentioning that the invention of *writing* is both expressive of and instrumental to the move from immediacy to abstract thought.

In ancient Israel, too, the mind at a certain time rose above the stage of mythical tribal gods to the idea of one true God high above the world with respect to whom all the other gods were false gods. Accordingly, the ultimately moral opposition of good versus evil (sin, Satan) also emerged in these times. And the rituals of sacrificial killings were now experienced as ungodly, because what God really wanted was the piety of the heart. This is the same dissolution of the immediacy of experience that was described for ancient Greece, although in a different way. The change here is not one from myth/ritual to philosophy, but to religion. However, the equally radical shift from myth and ritual to religion (the religious mode of being-in-the-world) is also a *logos* move, a manifestation of the logos, of the power of abstraction. The One God above the world objectively reflects the fact that the mind had pulled itself out of the ocean it had been floating in and become conscious of itself, thereby establishing itself as consciousness vis-à-vis the world.

In this new mode of being-in-the-world, which manifested itself in two different ways in ancient Greece and Israel, *the condition of the possibility of myth is passé*, although what I described briefly here is only the first immediacy of logos. The consciousness that emerged is not yet self-consciousness, has not become conscious of itself *as* consciousness and Subjectivity. This happened only during the latter period of Western history, during the time from, say, Nicholas of Cusa or Descartes to Hegel. With this development, the departure from myth becomes all the more radical and definitive: Inasmuch as consciousness has realized itself to be subjectivity, it has lost what was the very precondition of myth: the possibility to substantiate, hypostatize, project, personify. The semantic has been sublated and evaporated into syntax, the sensual content of the imaginal has been dissolved and liquefied into the logical form of the life of consciousness or of Subjectivity itself. After the world dominated by the image of the Father (e.g., Father Zeus), i.e., the philosophy of Antiquity, and after the age of the Son, i.e., medieval metaphysics, the third period of Western metaphysics is that age when it came home to consciousness that it is *Spirit*.

* * *

And yet this is not the last stage. In our brief review, we have witnessed the shift "from mythos to logos," "from nature to mind." And we have seen that this shift became possible only through the mind's tearing itself out of its being submerged in nature. What needs to be stressed here, however, is that it was the mind's, not man's, emancipation from nature. "Metaphysical *man*" (the successor to "mythological man") remained logically contained in nature and ultimately in God as the ground of nature. The fundamental human embeddedness in nature endured. Nature remained the horizon of metaphysical thought. Indeed, the *logos*, the *mens,* was the logos or mind of the *world*, not the mind of an atomic individual. In other words, only within nature had the mind freed itself from nature; it had become mind, but it stayed "natural mind."[8] But with the modern period, starting with the 19th century, this, too, changed. In Schopenhauer's *The World as Will and Idea* (1819) we may have the first major document of the soul that shows that "metaphysical man" has been replaced by "*psychological* man," for whom truth, if it still exists for him at all, resides in *his* personal ideas about the world. We could describe this shift with the formula, "from logos or mind to person." Now the embeddedness in nature is over for man himself, *existentially*, which shows above all in the economic sphere: in the radical change from the craft and small manufactory mode of production to industrial production, for which nature has no dignity in itself any more, but is fundamentally reduced to a source of raw materials.

A brief list of some of the major changes that happened with the fundamental rupture between the age of metaphysics and that of modernity suffices here. These changes include:

- the center has been lost altogether,
- the individual has fallen out of its containment in religion and metaphysics, which were essentially communal knowledge, and has thereby turned into an essentially private, atomic individual,

---

[8] We may also think here of Pseudo-Democritus's axiom of nature (cf. *CW* 16 § 469): "nature delights in nature, nature conquers nature, nature enjoys its mastery over nature." Nature remains here, for the metaphysical mind, the unsurpassable limit and horizon. The radical changes are nevertheless only inner-natural changes.

THE HISTORICITY OF MYTH

- man therefore feels fundamentally alienated and is all of a sudden captivated by *existential(ist) worries and subject to neurotic disorders,*
- faith and knowledge have consequently split apart,
- the mind has left the stage of self-consciousness, having seen through its ideas (conceptions, *Vorstellungen) as our ideas and thus ultimately as a language game,*
- the arts have demonstrated that truth is essentially irrepresentable (*unanschaulich*), if there should still exist such a thing as truth at all,
- under these circumstances "*metaphysical*" satisfaction can be had only through *paradis artificiels* (Baudelaire), i.e., through drugs of whatever sort.

In modernity, myth has become abstract twice over, totally divorced from its native mode of being-in-the-world. Precisely because it is abstract, thoroughly obsolete and harmless, it could be rediscovered for our time and can be indulged in as one of these drugs, a drug of a spiritual or psychological, not of a physiological or chemical nature. It can also be fair game for exploitation by the advertising industry for its purposes to interest consumers in certain products. And it can also be used by the mind as material to soberly study its own history and nature.

But what it cannot be any more is myth.

CHAPTER FOUR

Interiorizing Psychology into Itself: Following the Movement from Kant to Hegel in the Background of Giegerich's Psychology Project

GREG MOGENSON

Pushing Off

Let us begin with a brief summary of the lectures we heard yesterday. In the first of these, "'Conflict/Resolution,' 'Opposites/Creative Union' versus Dialectics, and the Climb Up the Slippery Mountain," Dr. Giegerich introduced us to the topic of dialectical thinking. A main point of that lecture was that dialectics does not start out with two opposing or conflicting figures which it then reconciles, but rather, "with one single idea, notion, phenomenon and then shows its internal contradiction." In his second lecture, "Different Moments of Truth," Giegerich further defined his approach to interpretation through reference to the Kantian distinction between analytic and synthetic judgments:

> Inasmuch as my reading of myth is a psychological one and I define psychology as the discipline of interiority, my thinking about myth obviously has to be analytical in this [Kantian] sense. It cannot be synthetic, because if it were synthetic, it

would think of something that has something literally outside itself, a literal Other, and then it ipso facto would be thinking in terms of *external* relations between two or more things or persons. But for psychology there is no Other. Or the other that there is is the soul's own other, its internal other, that is to say, itself *as* other.[1]

Following upon this brief indication of his interpretative stance, Dr. Giegerich provided a penetrating analysis of the dialectical movement inherent in several myths. Even without that fascinating application of theory to practice, however, the above-cited passage already tells us much about the larger aspect of his psychology project. I refer here to the fact that in these few sentences Giegerich no sooner mentions Kant's judgments than he pushes off from them into the more Hegelian mode of thought that he had introduced us to in his first lecture. Now, with this move, it could be said, Giegerich retraces a step already taken in the history of philosophy, the step that Hegel took to become Kant's dialectical successor. Looking back, this is a comparison that can be drawn. But, of course, Giegerich takes this step today, not for the field of philosophy, but for psychology. And the upshot of this is that it is no longer Kant who is dialectically succeeded, but Jung.[2]

Aptly dubbed a psychologist of the future and philosopher of the past,[3] Jung, it will be recalled, repeatedly proclaimed his affinity with Kant while making just as plain his antipathy for that "psychologist *manqué*,"[4] as he called him, Hegel. Decrying what he called "the victory of Hegel over Kant," Jung opined that this movement "dealt the gravest blow to reason and to the further development of the German and, ultimately, of the European mind …."[5] This, he believed,

---

[1] This volume, p. 26.
[2] For Giegerich's view of the Kant-Hegel-Jung problematic see his papers, "The Rescue of the World: Jung, Hegel, and the Subjective Universe," *Spring 1987: An Annual of Archetypal Psychology and Jungian Thought* (Dallas: Spring Publications, 1987), pp. 107-114; "Jung's Betrayal of his Truth: The Adoption of a Kant-based Empiricism and the Rejection of Hegel's Speculative Thought," *Harvest: Journal of Jungian Studies*, 44.1 (1990): 46-64.
[3] Stephanie de Voogd, "C. G. Jung: Psychologist of the Future, 'Philosopher' of the Past," *Spring 1977: An Annual of Archetypal Psychology and Jungian Thought* (Zürich: Spring Publications, 1977), pp. 175-182.
[4] C. G. Jung, *Letters, vol. 1: 1906-1950*, ed. G. Adler and A. Jaffé, tr. R. F. C. Hull (Princeton: Princeton University Press, 1973), p. 1944.
[5] C. G. Jung, *Collected Works*, tr. R. F. C. Hull (Princeton: Princeton University Press, 1953), vol. 8, para. 358 (all subsequent references to Jung's *Collected Works*, abbreviated to *CW* will be by volume and paragraph number, designated by §).

was "all the more dangerous as Hegel was a psychologist in disguise who projected great truths out of the subjective sphere into a cosmos he had himself created."[6] Adding further to this invective a few paragraphs later, Jung continues:

> A philosophy like Hegel's is a self-revelation of the psychic background and, philosophically, a presumption. Psychologically, it amounts to an invasion by the unconscious. The peculiar high-flown language Hegel uses bears out this view: it is reminiscent of the megalomanic language of schizophrenics, who use terrific spellbinding words to reduce the transcendent to subjective form, to give banalities the charm of novelty, or to pass off commonplaces as searching wisdom. So bombastic a terminology is a symptom of weakness, ineptitude, and lack of substance. But that does not prevent the latest German philosophy from using the same crackpot power-words and pretending that it is not unintentional psychology.[7]

A moment ago I quoted Giegerich's statement that "for psychology there is no other." Perhaps Jung's rejection of Hegel can be understood in the light of this principle. Perhaps, that is to say, Jung had had to reject the philosophy of Hegel because as philosophy it had the form of an external other. But here we must remember the second part of Giegerich's statement. Immediately after telling us that for psychology there is no other, Giegerich added the important caveat, " Or the other that there is is the soul's own other, its internal other, that is to say, itself *as* other." Now Jung was no stranger to the notion of internal others; indeed, his entire work springs from what might justly be called a vis-à-vis with a whole series of inner, contradictory others, be these the figures of dream and fantasy or persons from the social world who have been invested with unconscious significance via projection.[8] It might have been expected that Jung, the originator of the concept of the shadow,[9] would have recognized in Hegel the internal other of his own psychology project. Certainly his references

---

[6] Jung, *CW* 8, § 358.
[7] *Ibid.*, § 360.
[8] Renos Papadopoulos, "Jung and the Concept of the Other," in R. Papadopoulos & G. Saayman, eds., *Jung in Modern Perspective: The Master and his Legacy* (Dorset: Prism Press, 1991), pp. 54-88.
[9] Jung, *CW* 9ii, § 13-19.

to Hegel as a "psychologist *manqué*" and to Hegelian philosophy as "unintentional psychology" point in this direction. But as Jung's derisive tone makes clear, Hegel was a shadow figure that he could not integrate. The irony here is compelling. By Jung's own lights, we who follow after him must recognize in the Hegel he so adamantly rejected a most important figure for the further development of his thought.

Muddying the Waters

These words of summary and quotations from Jung are enough to indicate our task this morning, which is to grapple with this movement from Kant to Hegel that plays in the background of the psychological approach to interpretation that Dr. Giegerich has presented. I say "grapple," here, because a true sense of what is at stake in this movement can be acquired only through struggle and effort. It is not enough to simply quote the ideas that are involved; we must delve into them, following the logic of their twists and turns. As I am sure most of you will have often experienced, there is a great deal of eyebrow furrowing that can be called for in such an undertaking. Again and again the challenge of thought must be met with burning concentration. At other times, a softer focus is needed to capture the whole of a movement, the whole of thought, even if only in a very sketchy way at first.

Speaking for myself, I can certainly tell you that I have not been without such vicissitudes in preparing my lecture for this seminar. Singling out one of these, I will mention that a concern welled up in me upon first reading a draft of Dr. Giegerich's lectures, a worry, really, that my cogitations might "muddy the waters." A practising analyst, I spend the majority of my time listening to patients. Myth in the formal sense claims my attention only once in a while in a free hour. The same can be said for philosophy. As a result of this, my knowledge of these fields is a muddy mixture at best. Indeed, what Jung said of the archetypes—that they are not isolated monads, but exist "in a state of contamination of the most complete mutual interpenetration and interfusion"[10]—pretty much sums up the state of my knowledge of myth and philosophy. In my mind, Oedipus could find himself making

---

[10] C. G. Jung, *The Integration of the Personality*, tr. Stanley Dell (London: Kegan & Paul, 1940), p. 91.

Kierkegaard's "leap of faith" in the magic sandals of Hermes, Odin riding the winged Pegasus! It all depends on what the patient resonates for me on the mythological and philosophical axes of what might be called, after Bion, my Jungian grid.[11] And so it is that I ask myself what I have to offer to serious students of myth.

Uncertain as I am about addressing this seminar, I have nevertheless accepted the challenge to do so, encouraged by an interpretive principle that is central to the interpretation of both myth and psychological phenomena in general. This principle, which stems from a remark Jung makes with respect to the technique of active imagination, is frequently cited by Dr. Giegerich as being central to his own approach: "Above all, don't let anything from outside, that does not belong, get into it, for the fantasy-image has 'everything it needs.'"[12] Recalling this principle in relation to my fantasy-image of muddying the waters, it occurs to me that I might approach my concern, my worry, dialectically, "reflecting it into itself," as Giegerich would say. Perhaps, if I simply stay within my limits as practising analyst, and more immediately still, within my anxiety about "muddying the waters," everything needed will be there. Seconding this thought, an alchemical adage that Jung may well have been alluding to when he stated his interpretive principle comes to mind: "This stinking water contains everything it needs."[13] If this is so of stinking water (i.e., fantasy) then why not also of muddy water?

Kant's Judgments

Giegerich begins his lecture, "Different Moments of Truth," with the aforementioned reference to Kant's distinction between analytic and synthetic judgments. Desiring a fuller understanding of these terms, which I had not thought about in many years, I turned to the philosophy texts of my school days. At the risk of adding even further mud to the mix, I would like to begin my presentation today

---

[11] Wilfred Bion, "The Grid" (1977) in his *Two Papers* (London: Karnac Books, 1989).
[12] Jung, *CW* 14, § 749. For a discussion of this principle by Giegerich see his "Comment on, 'The Autonomous Psyche: A Communication to Goodheart from the Bi-Personal Field of Paul Kugler and James Hillman'," in *Spring 1985: An Annual of Archetypal Psychology and Jungian Thought* (Dallas: Spring Publications), pp. 172-174. See also his *The Soul's Logical Life: Towards a Rigorous Notion of Psychology* (Frankfurt am Main: Peter Lang GmbH, 1998), p. 126.
[13] Jung, *CW* 16, § 454.

by sharing something of what I gleaned from this exercise. Following upon this I shall, in my second lecture, discuss what I consider to be the four key moments of Giegerich's dialectic of interpretation.

The Analytic and Synthetic, the A Priori *and the* A Posteriori

According to Kant, every proposition that we make, every judgment, is either analytic or synthetic. In the philosopher's own words,

> In all judgements in which the relation of a subject to a predicate is thought ... this relation is possible in two different ways. Either the predicate B belongs to the subject A, as something which is (covertly) contained in this concept A; or B lies outside the concept A, although it does indeed stand in connection with it. In the one case I call the judgement *analytic* and the other *synthetic*.[14]

Briefly explicating Kant's distinction, Giegerich explains that in analytic judgment-type statements, "the predicate tells you what is already contained in the subject." Statements of this kind, he reminds us, elucidate the meaning of their own initial terms, but supply no further information. They are definitional, conceptual, tautological. As an example he gives the statement, "all bodies are extended." That bodies are extended is essential to the definition of body. There is no body that is not extended. Furthermore, no search for a body that is an exception to the rule is required to ascertain that this judgment is true. Logically, the idea of a body that lacks extension is a contradiction of the very idea of a body. It simply makes no sense. Synthetic judgments, on the other hand, are entirely different. In them the predicate supplies additional information, as in the statement "some bodies are light." Judgments of this kind are empirical. Some are so in the sense that they have simply been abstracted from sensory impressions; others in the sense that, already and in advance of such sensory experience, they bring to bear the apperceptive presuppositions through which the data of the senses is combined to produce our phenomenal world picture. The statement, "every change has a cause," is an example of this second, "transcendental"

---

[14] Cited in S. Körner, *Kant* (Harmondsworth: Penguin Books, 1955), pp. 18-19.

or constituting sense of the empirical. The addition that it brings as its predicate—the reference to "cause"—comes, not from the world as it is in itself (according to Kant we cannot know the world *per se*), but from the side of the subject. And here let us note that it was in response to Hume's sceptical conclusion that causality could not be accounted for rationally that Kant affirmed the objective reality of the concept of cause as it pertains to objects of experience, demonstrating at the same time its origin from pure understanding, without prior experimental or empirical input.

Now in Kant's terminology the difference that I have just touched upon in connection to the two kinds of synthetic judgment-type statements has to do with what he calls the *a posteriori* and the *a priori* character of the judgments in general. Whether analytic or synthetic, a judgment (we could also say, a thought) has an *a priori* character when it is at once both necessary and universal. With reference to these criteria, Kant writes: "First, if we meet a proposition which in being thought is thought as having *necessity* [in the sense that its negation would be a contradiction in terms] then it is a judgement *a priori*. Second: … If a judgement is thought in strict universality, then it is not derived from experience, but *a priori* valid."[15] In contrast to judgments with an *a priori* character, those with an *a posteriori* character consist of descriptive accounts of particular experiences or sense impressions. The statement, "all bodies, if deprived of support, fall downwards,"[16] readily conveys what is intended here.

Bringing the two sets of terms together gives further definition to the judgments. For Kant, these fall into three kinds—analytic *a priori*, synthetic *a posteriori*, and synthetic *a priori*. Of these, it is the last mentioned, synthetic *a priori*-type statements, that are the most important for Kant philosophically, because in them the shaping influence of the mind's own categories upon the raw elements of sense perception—what has been called "Kant's Copernican revolution"—is disclosed. Doubtless, it is statements and thought-forms of this kind that Jung had in mind when he defined his archetypes as the imaginal equivalents of Kant's logical categories.[17] Like synthetic *a priori* judgments, the Jungian archetype also combines experience with something categorical that precedes experience in a shaping way.

---

[15] Cited in Körner, *Kant*, p. 24.
[16] Körner, *Kant*, p. 20.
[17] Cf. Jung *CW* 10 § 14; *CW* 9, i § 136n, 150; *CW* 8 § 840; *CW* 3 § 527.

But has something been left out here? In combining the terms analytic and synthetic with *a priori* and *a posteriori,* should there not also be a fourth possibility? What about analytic *a posteriori*-type judgments? With a little reflection we can understand with Kant the impossibility of this fourth kind of judgment. Analytic statements, being strictly concerned with the meaning of their own terms, cannot be formulated in combination with *a posteriori*-type statements, which are based, not on logic, but experience.[18] This being so, the coupling of the two is neither permissible nor possible. Putting this issue in terms of Jung's interpretive principle (if only to keep this principle present in our minds), we can say that anything of an *a posteriori* character, that is, any sensory observation or empirical detail, is incompatible with an analytic judgment, as such observations and details would amount to our letting something from outside the self-referential analytic judgment, which does not belong to it, get into it. Seeing may be believing, as the old adage declares, but knowing in the sense of Kant's *a priori*-type judgments is not a function of ocular witness. Like alchemy's "stinking water," such judgments, whether analytic or synthetic, have everything they need within themselves to insight their own truth. They are sufficient unto themselves.

From Synthetic Judgments to the Analytic Retort

The repetition that I have just made of my earlier reference to "stinking waters" may return us to the problem of "muddying the waters." How, it may reasonably be asked, does this statement fit into our discussion of Kant's judgments?

Like many life phenomena, this anxiety of mine has the form of a *synthetic judgment*. The muddy quality referred to in the predicate of the sentence, "the water is muddy," is something additional to the simple, elemental meaning of water. Far from being necessary or universal, it delimits, qualifies, and empirically observes the particular character of the water to which it refers. Now, for chemistry and biology, synthetic *a posteriori* observations of this kind are just what is sought. Indeed, they are the form in which the vast array of empirical data is represented in the course of scientific research—or so the natural sciences in their pursuit of objectivity have somewhat

---

[18] Cited in Körner, *Kant*, p. 20.

naively believed. But as Kant has shown, the empirically-observing mind is not merely the passive register of information received from without. Rather, it actively forms the information conveyed to it via the senses into cognitively amenable representations by means of such transcendental categories as quality, quantity, relation, modality and the various sub-categories of these.

Now Kant's account of the active contribution that the mind makes to the categorizing of its own experiential picture of the world could be said to be a most important precursor of modern psychology in general and of the depth psychologies in particular. This is certainly the case with Jung's analytical psychology. Bringing something of the Kantian philosophy in which he had been reared to bear upon the interpretation of myth, Jung writes, "It is not storms, not thunder and lightning, not rain and cloud that remain as images in the psyche, but the fantasies caused by the affects they arouse. ... Man's curses against devastating thunderstorms, his terror of the unchained elements—these affects anthropomorphize the passions of nature, and the purely physical element becomes an angry god."[19] Like the myths to which it has so often turned for its models, depth psychology is rooted, not in images that are derived *reproductively* or *a posteriori* from the world—the storms, thunder, and lightning mentioned by Jung—but, rather, in an *a priori* (Jung would say, archetypal) *productive* factor. Explaining this further in a letter, Jung writes that "... images are surely answers to external facts and conditions, but they are *the answers of the psyche* and therefore produce accurate pictures of the psychic facts. If you compare the sun-myth to the actual experience of the senses, then you see the whole difference. The conscious mind perceives the sun as a round celestial body, the unconscious produces a myth which in its imagery has nothing but a very faint relation with the actual perception of the senses."[20]

Doubtless, Jung's contribution here is an advance over some of the more simplistic psychologies of his time that regarded the mind as being more simply reproductive. Looking back from our present vantage point, however, it is just as evident that this advance did not go far enough. Pushing off from Jung, Giegerich, as we shall see, would have

---

[19] Jung, *CW* 8 § 331.
[20] Jung, *Letters*, vol. 1, p. 199.

us overcome Jung's distinction between "the psyche," on the one hand, and "external facts and conditions," on the other, by thinking of the latter as no more than the already interiorized material of "the soul's" self-display.[21] Jung, as the texts I have just cited clearly indicate, set up his psychology in terms of a positive outside that is the foil, as it were, of an equally positive inside. Styling himself as an empiricist of the psyche, he endeavoured to turn his empiricist lens around, focusing it upon the contribution that the psyche makes to perception. Expressing this in terms of Kant's judgments, it can be said that he looked at what was analytic and *a priori* from a synthetic and *a posteriori* vantage point. He looked, that is to say, from outside, as if the psyche's categories were objects in front of him.

Critical of Jung's approach (which is at once both indicative of and incompatible with Jung's own recognition of psychology's lack of an Archimedean position outside the psyche from which to view it), Giegerich would have us go the other way, the way of entering into the phenomenon in question in such a way that the *a priori* intensiveness of thought may fathom the logic of that phenomenon from within. Applying this to the matter at hand, that is, to my worry about "muddying the waters," the challenge becomes one of dialectically reflecting the synthetic judgment-type statement, "the water is muddy," into itself as an analytic judgment by taking it reflexively, hermeneutically, psychologically.

But how can this be done? According to Kant the only way to demonstrate the psychological aspect of such a statement would be to show that what it brings in its predicate is from the side of the mind. This, however, cannot really be shown. Though there are Jungians aplenty who would speak out of Jung's errant Kantianism of a "mud archetype," with a moment's reflection we realize that "mud" is not to be found in Kant's system alongside the transcendental concepts and intuitions through which the mind constructs our experience of causality and our perception of time and space. It is not, that is to say, the *a priori* category of a synthetic *a priori* judgment, let alone of an analytic one. On the contrary, as far as water is concerned, what muddies it is contingent—the predicate, properly speaking, of a synthetic *a posteriori* judgment.

---

[21] Personal communication.

Or is it? Reading Kant against the grain, let us consider giving an analytic reading to what seems to be a straightforward empirical statement. On this account, we would say that when absolutely fathomed, water cannot be other than muddy. Or putting this another way, that the essence of water can only be the context that sullies it, the mud that makes it real. Now clearly, the thought that is required to think the necessity of muddied water is very different from the Kantian type of thinking that so cleanly divides subject from predicate that a subjectively conditioned phenomenal world picture is divided off from the world of reality as it is in itself and which we can never know as such.

Discipline of Interiority

Before pressing on with a logical analysis of my muddy water, a few words about psychology. As defined by Giegerich, psychology is the discipline of interiority. Using this analytic *a priori*-type position as a hermeneutic of interiorization or notional mirror we can take any statement and reflectively constitute consciousness within or through it in such a manner that, in the case of synthetic judgment-type statements, the predicated phenomena at hand are no longer merely externally in front of consciousness, but rather, come home to themselves as consciousness, i.e., the form as which knowing from within occurs. Putting this another way, we could say that psychology constitutes itself by reflecting any phenomenon more deeply into itself in terms of the aforementioned notional mirror. Or again that psychology, as the "discipline of interiority," analytically interiorizes synthetic statements (both *a priori* and *a posteriori*) into themselves as if these were the immanently posited predicate or internal other of the analytic *a priori*-type judgment that psychology within itself can be said to be.

But here, now, have I not muddied the philosophical waters? Like Oedipus wearing the winged sandals of Hermes, is Kant, as I am now presenting him, not wearing Hegel's monocle? Lest I here fall foul of the adage that a little undergraduate knowledge of philosophy is a dangerous thing, I should emphasize that with my idea of approaching synthetic judgments as if they were analytic ones, we have really left Kant's analysis of the judgments for Hegel's axiom of internal relations. According to

Hegel's axiom, every subject meets itself, its own *internal* other, in any and all things, any and all predicates, for at its most concrete every subject (proposition, statement, judgment) is 'angelogically contextualized' by, and itself the ground or context for, everything else, subject or object. Now, the implication of this sublated vision is that the constraints that Kant placed upon knowing do not apply. For when dialectically deployed the stoppered retort of the analytic *a priori* mode of reflection has a transgressive, penetrating propensity which, contrary to Kant's own view, obtains real knowledge even as in the fullness of the Hegelian vision it cancels the distinction Kant drew between the phenomenal and noumenal realms. In the 'sand play' of the world, everything can be known from within, i.e., subjectively and self-consciously as self-relation. The distinction, 'subject' and 'object,' is cancelled and overcome.

Clear as Mud

So, again, what can be done with regard to my trepidation about muddying the waters? How might this worry be interiorized into itself, this resistance worked though?

In the first place, the empirico-literalist in me needs to realize that the statement is not a synthetic *a posteriori*-type judgment, but a metaphor. While it certainly has the semblance of a synthetic *a posteriori* judgment, we can readily understand that the statement does not refer, in the manner of Kantian empiricism, to an external relation, water and mud. On the contrary, its predicate, far from bringing information that is additional to the subject, is the subject's own presentation of itself to itself as something else, the external having been left behind. Said another way (and here again we take the Hegelian tack), intrinsically and at its most concrete the subject of such a statement is the inner unity of itself and that which external reflection would regard as additional or external to it. And now we must add: as vast as the difference between the subject and its predicate other may seem, this difference, at bottom, is only the difference between implicitness and explicitness.

Just here, an insight dawns. Without its other the subject could not manifest itself in the fullness of its finite infinitude. Or to say the same thing in terms of my specimen concern, without some mud in the mix, "water" could be nothing more than a worrisome droplet on the periodic table of Plato's heaven—unreal, irrepresentable, and abstract.

I spoke at the outset of an interpretive principle that Giegerich has taken over from Jung (and Jung before him from alchemy), the one that states that the fantasy-image has everything it needs within itself to become itself more fully. Entering the dialectical movement that this principle unfurls, it can now be understood that the "water" referred to in my worry about "muddying the waters" is used in the sense of "clear." It is a pictorial representation of the idea of clarity. And along with this comes the realization that clarity's other is unclarity, opaqueness, muddy waters. True to Jung's point that consciousness cannot exist "without the perception of differences,"[22] clarity cannot be known apart from the inchoate foils of its fathoming. For the clear by itself would indicate a dazzling, blinding, bad-infinity kind of abstract lucidity. But the whole point of clarity is to *become clear,* to clarify something that is unclear, muddy. We do not have clarity—just like that. Such naive clarity must slip back—like the brothers climbing the glass mountain in the fairy tale discussed by Dr. Giegerich—if it is to bring *real* clarity and not merely an unsullied, narcissistically encapsulated pristine abstraction.

In connection to these reflections, I am reminded of a statement of Jung's and a passage from Nietzsche. In his *Alchemical Studies* Jung writes: "One does not become enlightened by imagining figures of light, but by making the darkness conscious."[23] Notice that the light referred to here, like the clarity we just discussed, cannot be had without an encounter with the darkness that is its other. Nietzsche makes a similar point. In a beautiful passage titled, "And once more Grow Clear," that most psychological of philosophers compares himself and his favoured readers to "open fountains [who] would hinder no one from drinking from us." Complicating this is the fact that, for that very reason, we also "have no means of preventing ourselves from being made *turbid* and dark, ...

> no means of preventing the age in which we live casting its "up-to-date rubbish" into us, or of hindering filthy birds throwing their excrement, the boys their trash, and the fatigued resting

---
[22] Jung, *CW* 14, § 603.
[23] Jung, *CW* 13, § 265-266.

travellers their misery, great and small, into us. But we do as we have always done: we take whatever is cast into us down into our depths—for we are deep, we do not forget—*and once more grow clear* ....[24]

Like Nietzsche's fountain taking whatever is cast into it down into its depths and once more growing clear, psychology, as what Giegerich calls the discipline of interiority, takes all manner of phenomena into itself even as it constitutes itself by reflecting these into themselves in an enlightening way. Made turbid and dark by what in their first immediacy seem to be external objects and relations, it keeps to its program of not letting "anything from outside, that does not belong to it, get into it." This is not to say that it hinders anything or anyone from drinking from it. Still less that it pulls back from life, unsullied and aloof. Psychology as the discipline of interiority is not a solipsistic retreat from the world. The point, rather, is that while allowing itself to be permeated by the situation in which it finds itself, it simultaneously lavishes its thinking substance upon the phenomenon-at-hand even as, by both succumbing to and rejecting the seduction theory each phenomenon brings, it takes these as the internal other of its own self-relation. Of such is the hermeneutic through which it "once more grows clear."[25]

Negating the Philosophers

I would like to bring these muddy musings to a close by "growing clear" with respect to a final issue. I refer here to the whole set-up of my presentation as this is indicated in the title of my talk. The problem is not with the main part, "Interiorizing Psychology into

---

[24] Friedrich Nietzsche, *The Joyful Wisdom*, tr. Thomas Common (New York: Frederick Ungar Publishing, 1960), p. 346.

[25] Further to these reflections, I think we can look again at analytic *a posteriori* judgments. Are these truly as impossible as Kant maintained? Moving from Kant's clearly delineated judgments to Hegel's axiom of internal relations, does it not become evident that the analytic subject would be merely abstract without the *a posteriori* as its predicate? While it is certainly true that the analytic, being entirely a function of its own self-defining logic, is contradicted by the *a posteriori*, which is drawn from experience, this contradiction can also be comprehended as a self-contradiction that opens each into the other as its own *internal* other. Putting this another way, when we push off from Kant's reasoning with regard to the impossibility of analytic *a posteriori* judgments, we come to Hegel's notion of the "existing CONCEPT" which has the form of a judgment absolved from the difference between analytic and *a posteriori*, subject and object, individual and universal, one and many.

Itself," which well enough conveys the essence of Giegerich's project. The problem lies rather in the announcement given in the subtitle that we shall be "Following the Movement from Kant to Hegel in the Background of Giegerich's Psychology Project." As didactically valuable as it is to delve into this movement (Giegerich has done so himself many times in his writings), it also involves us in a contradiction. Putting this it terms of the passage from Nietzsche that I just quoted above, for a psychology that defines itself as the discipline of interiority, and which thinks exclusively in terms of internal relations, Kant and Hegel are as flotsam in its fountain. This is not to say that as analytical psychologists we do not need to fathom the consequences of Jung's having undialectically sided with the one philosopher against the other. On the contrary, comprehending these is an important task. The problem, rather, lies in my having gotten into the philosophical issues that concerned Kant and Hegel to the extent that I have. This, I now see, may have had the effect of setting them up as external facts, as if nothing more were at stake for us here than pushing off from Kant and applying Hegel. Our commitment, however, is not to philosophy and its issues in their positivity, but to psychology in its negativity as reflection into itself. What Hegel or anyone else from any other disciple has contributed to their respective fields is important to us *within psychology* only insofar as it provides us with ideas of how to handle our own, strictly psychological concerns.[26] Thus, when we take up Kant, Hegel and their ilk, it must be understood that we do so only as they are already interiorized. Whatever they are for philosophy, for us they are at most valued figures in our sand play of interiority. "We have to understand," writes Giegerich, "that psychology is the study of the reflections in some mirror and not the study of what the mirror is a reflection of. This turn to the already reflected is not a trick to get at the otherwise invisible soul after all, and not a second-best substitute for 'the real thing.' On the contrary, we know that the already reflected is psychology's 'real thing.'"[27]

---

[26] Wolfgang Giegerich, personal communication.
[27] Wolfgang Giegerich, "Is the Soul 'Deep?' Entering and Following the Logical Movement of Heraclitus' 'Fragment 45,'" *Spring 64: A Journal of Archetype and Culture* (Woodstock, CT: Spring Journal, 1998), p. 2.

CHAPTER FIVE

Different Moments in Dialectical Movement

GREG MOGENSON

In my earlier presentation, as part of an attempt to follow the movement from Kant to Hegel that plays in the background of Giegerich's critique of Jung, I also approached a simple life phenomenon—my own worry about "muddying the waters"—in the spirit of Giegerich's approach to interpretation as this has come across to me from his lectures to this seminar and from my familiarity with his other writings. Turning this around, I propose that we now look, not at the dialectical movement of some particular statement, issue, image or concern, but at some of the important moments within the dialectical mode of interpretation itself. These I will discuss under four headings: Prime Matter, Contradiction and Negation, Negation of the Negation, and Absolute Negative Interiorization. Following upon these discussions I will then, by way of conclusion, reflect upon Giegerich's notion of "true psychology."

Prime Matter

The chief merit of the dialectical approach is that it can begin anywhere with anything. The starting point could be a statement, an idea, an assertion, a dream, a life event, a text or document. The only proviso to this is that it must be a real and pressing concern which consciousness works upon with wholehearted dedication, sublating it from the outset, as it were. Borrowing a term from alchemy, Giegerich speaks of this sublated starting point as the "prima materia" or "prime matter." For the alchemists (as for Aristotle and the pre-Socratics before them) the prime matter was the one basic substance underlying all others. On this account, it was regarded as the basis of the transformation process. As one alchemical author expresses this, "... metals cannot be changed into gold or silver before being reduced to their primary matter."[1]

Now for the purposes of our discussion, it is important to appreciate that the idea of reducing the variety of the world's substances to one is not given by the senses. It must be thought. Innocent of the concentrated parsimony of the mind (though fully assisted by the synthetic *a priori* concepts and intuitions discussed by Kant), the senses instill in us the impression of a world that is diverse and manifold. And following upon this, the resemblance-seeking psyche kindles a light in the midst this diversity. Drawing comparisons between one thing and another, it allows us to discern what things are *like*. But these nascent forms of consciousness are not yet the crowning awareness that can think the eachness of every finite thing in the light of its being at the same time a moment of the infinite, a manifestation of the all. Consciousness in this sense must be acquired through the labour of its constituting notion. And for such an opus to succeed it must begin with a substance, or rather, with a conception of substance, in which what we may variously refer to as the subject, consciousness, spirit, mind and soul is already present, or at least nascently so.

A question arises. Is the prime matter fashioned or is it found? The similarity of this question to one that has been raised by D. W. Winnicott brings resonances from contemporary psychoanalysis into our discussion.

---

[1] Fugulus, *A Golden and Blessed Casket of Nature's Marvels*, p. 298, cited in Edward Edinger, *The Anatomy of the Psyche: Alchemical Symbolism in Psychotherapy* (La Salle, Il.: Open Court, 1985), p. 10.

Through Winnicott's work, psychoanalysis has come to know the prime matter of the soul's making by the names "transitional object" and "transitional phenomena."[2] Observing children at play with a favoured object (or on a whole other level, man at play in his religion and culture[3]), we find ourselves tempted to ask—were these objects created or discovered? Vaguely aware that to ask such a question would be to bring the wrong kind of enlightenment to bear upon the process, we instinctively know that we must keep it to ourselves. It was the same with the alchemists. Speaking to both possibilities (while leaving the question unasked), some authors refer to creating the prime matter, others to finding it. The following passage is representative of the latter possibility.

> This Matter lies before the eyes of all; everybody sees it, touches it, loves it, but knows it not. It is glorious and vile, precious and of small account, and is found everywhere. ...
> To be brief, our Matter has as many names as there are things in the world; that is why the foolish know it not.[4]

We said above that the dialectic can start with anything. Further to this point, we mentioned the vital objects of transitional space. Whether these are the playthings of children, the forms of mankind's cultural life, or a worry about muddying the waters, we know that they can be immensely varied. In keeping with this, the prime matter is described in the passage from the alchemical text which we have just cited as being utterly ubiquitous. Having "as many names as there are things in the world," it, too, can be "found everywhere." An implication of this is that the object or issue at hand—whatever it may be—is raised on account of its absolute finitude or particularity to the power of the infinite. Underscoring this, the dialectical nature of the prime matter, the alchemist avers that "it is glorious and vile, precious and of small account ...."

Before moving on to the next moment in what I am calling the dialectic of interpretation, let us briefly examine another alchemical

---

[2] Donald W. Winnicott, "Transitional Objects and Transitional Phenomena," *Playing and Reality* (London: Tavistock Publications, 1971), pp. 1-25.
[3] Cf. Donald W. Winnicott, "The Location of Cultural Experience," *Playing and Reality*, pp. 95-103.
[4] A. E. Waite, trans., *The Hermetic Museum* 1:13, cited in Edinger, *The Anatomy of the Psyche*, p. 11.

description of the prime matter. As will be immediately recognized, this passage, representative of those that refer to *making* the prime matter,[5] has been chosen on account of its likeness to Jung's interpretive principle, "Above all, don't let anything from outside, that does not belong, get into it, for the fantasy-image has 'everything it needs.'"[6] Also well conveyed in this passage is the latency of the goal of the opus—the *lapis* or philosopher's stone—in the initial material.

> As concerns the [Prime] Matter, it is *one*; and contains within itself all that is needed. ... In the same way Arnold of Villa Nova writes in his "Flower of Flowers": "Our stone is made out of one thing, and with one thing." To the same effect he says to the King of Naples: "All that is in our stone is essential to it, nor does it need any foreign ingredient. Its nature is one, and it is *one* thing."[7]

This text needs little in the way of elucidation. I will only reflect further on Jung's interpretive principle in the light of it. Jung's warning—"above all, don't let anything from outside, that does not belong, get into it"—may suggest to some a defensive sort of closure. In his review of Jung's autobiography, Winnicott objected to the closure that he felt was implied by Jung's interest in mandalas.[8] Something of the same order may be suspected here—a fear of contamination or of penetration perhaps. But this would be to read Jung weakly. More deeply comprehended, Jung's cautionary rhetoric is a negative presentation of the idea of inclusion. Following the dialectical movement inherent in his statement, we can say that nothing from outside can get in, not because it is being kept out, but because the distinction between outside and inside has been overcome. The prime matter "is *one*, and contains within itself all that is needed." Likewise, for Jung "the fantasy-image has 'everything it needs.'" This conception, this attitude, is itself the retort or alchemical *vas*. Unlike an actual glass vessel, which has a delimited, positive inside that contains only those contents that we literally place inside of it,

---

[5] It is the reference to the stone being made " ... *with* one thing" that implies the idea of production or making. The earlier part of the sentence, which refers to the stone as being "made *out of* one thing," indicates only *of what* the stone consists.

[6] C. G. Jung, *Collected Works*, tr. R. F. C. Hull, (Princeton: Princeton University Press, 1953), vol.14, para. 749 (all subsequent references to Jung's *Collected Works* will be by volume and paragraph number).

[7] Cited in Edinger, p. 11.

[8] Donald W. Winnicott, "Review of *Memories, Dreams, Reflections*," C. Winnicott, R. Shepherd, and M. Davis, eds., *Psycho-Analytic Explorations* (Cambridge, MA: Harvard University Press, 1989), pp. 482-492.

the *notional* vessel which is indicative of psychology is constituted by our thinking in each case the oneness of the prime matter or matter at hand in the light of its different moments. Leaping ahead to a formulation of Hegel's that Giegerich has carried forward into psychology, we could say of the prime matter, the *vas*, and the stone what the philosopher says of the absolute when he defines it as "the identity of identity and non-identity."[9] The identity of identity and non-identity is at once a definition of the *prima materia* and of the philosopher's stone, of both the beginning and the end. The ultimate formulation of how truth is constituted according to Hegelian philosophy, it is also the plaything of children.

Self-Contradiction and Negation

There are many approaches we could take in discussing this moment of the dialectic, as many as there are starting points for the dialectic itself. This being said, and in the interest of keeping the aforementioned movement beyond Kant to Hegel present to our minds, I propose that we briefly examine a small example of the self-contradictory work of the negative that is at play in this important transition.

Kant's critical philosophy, as I noted in my previous lecture, has been characterized as a "Copernican revolution." When this claim is taken as our *prima materia*, however, we find that it does not hold up. The crux of the matter is simply this: as radical as the Kantian revolution undoubtedly was in its psychologizing of the metaphysics that preceded it, it remained conservative in that it continued to uphold the principles of identity and of non-contradiction[10] that have been the mainstays of philosophical reasoning since Aristotle.[11] In light of

---

[9] Cf. G. W. F. Hegel: "But the Absolute itself is thus the identity of identity and non-identity, opposition and unity are both in it." Cited in Charles Taylor, *Hegel* (Cambridge: Cambridge University Press, 1975), p. 67.

[10] The Law of Identity holds that everything must be identical with itself ($X = X$). The Law of Contradiction (sometimes referred to as the Law of Non-contradiction) holds that nothing can be both itself and not itself (X and non-X). Both of these laws are considered to be primary laws of thought.

[11] Cf. G. W. F. Hegel: "Kant ... considers logic, that is, the aggregate of definitions and propositions which ordinarily passes for logic, to be fortunate in having attained so early to completion before the other sciences; since Aristotle, it has not lost any ground, but neither has it gained any, the latter because to all appearances it seems to be finished and complete. Now if logic has not undergone any change since Aristotle—and in fact, judging by modern compendiums of logic the changes frequently consist mainly in omissions—then surely the conclusion which should be drawn is that it is all the more in need of a total reconstruction; for spirit, after it labours over two thousand years,

this, the question arises: how can a revolution, especially a revolution as radical as the epithet "Copernican" suggests, still remain conservative? Is there not contradiction here, a negation even, of the epithet's superlative claim? That certainly is what Hegel would argue and what the movement beyond Kant (as the most recent exponent of traditional logic) to the dialectics of Hegel is about.

Now the point here, it is important to emphasis, is not to bring Kant down a peg or two by pointing out in an undialectical or pre-Hegelian manner that contradiction and non-identity figure in his work; rather, it is to raise these—contradiction and non-identity—up in our estimation. Hegel's rigorous and far-reaching re-introduction of philosophy's dialectical tradition into the philosophy of his period constituted a radical expansion of the reach of the mind beyond the limits set for it by formal logic and Enlightenment reason. And this expansion was made by a rescuing and retaining what traditional logic would undialectically disavow. Just as the stone that the builders rejected becomes the cornerstone of the new temple, according to a saying of Christ, so the Hegelian edifice of dialectical thinking constitutes itself out of what the builders of the older temple of traditional logic had regarded as the hallmarks of error and discarded on this account, contradiction and non-identity.[12]

This, of course, is to enormously condense a movement with many nuances. Painting with a broad brush, I have neglected to detail the recognition which Kant did give in his system to contradiction and dialectics. Let us at least touch on this in passing.

Appreciating the achievement of his predecessor, Hegel paid tribute to Kant as the one "more than any other, ... who resuscitated the name of

---

must have attained to a higher consciousness about its thinking and about is own pure, essential nature." *Hegel's Science of Logic*, tr. A.V. Miller (London: George Allen & Unwin, 1969), p. 51.

[12] Hegel did not deny the principles of traditional logic. When it is only a matter of formal logic these principles apply. With questions concerning the logic of reality, however, he maintained that formal logic is not adequate and that a dialectical approach is called for. In connection to my stating that "the Hegelian edifice of dialectical thinking constitutes itself out of what the builders of the older temple of traditional logic had regarded as the hallmarks of error," compare Hegel's call for a "total reconstruction" of traditional logic in the previous note.

Dialectic, and restored it to its post of honour."[13] This, according to Hegel, Kant had done " ... by working out the Antinomies of the reason."[14] But for Kant, the antinomies in which reason finds itself in contradiction with itself (antinomies such as "the world is at once limited in time and space and infinite" and "matter is made of discrete particles and is also a continuous composite") cannot be reconciled. And what's more, it is on account of these irreconcilable dialectics that he came to the conclusion that we cannot know reality as it is in itself, but only as it appears to us.

Now for Hegel the idea that we are barred from knowing reality by a phenomenal world picture constituted of the mind's own "dialectical illusions" was intolerable—and Kant's "Copernican revolution" more like an eclipse than a revolution.[15] Taking this problematic as his *prima materia*, Hegel reflected the antinomies that Kant had recognized into themselves, insisting that they can be reconciled. Kant's problem, in his view, was that each of the antinomies or "opposed moments" was taken by him "in isolation from the other," when, to a truer conception, " ... neither of these determinations taken alone, has truth; this belong[ing] only to their unity."[16] The real revolution was not in the mere recognition of antinomy or contradiction, important as this was. As we have just discussed, that led not to revolution, but eclipse. No, the more radical, or as one scholar of Hegel calls it, "mind-blowing"[17] move is to think in terms of the very self-contradictions and non-identities that had traditionally invalidated a proposition, disqualified a thought.

We may now return to the main line of our discussion. Squaring psychology with the Hegelian cornerstone of self-contradiction and non-identity (or more precisely with the cornerstone that is to be found in Hegel's definition of the absolute as "the identity of identity and

---

[13] G. W. F. Hegel, *Hegel's Logic*. Part one of *The Encyclopaedia of the Philosophical Sciences* (1830). tr. William Wallace (Oxford: Clarendon Press/OUP, 1975), p. 117.

[14] Hegel, *Hegel's Logic*, p. 117.

[15] Cf. Hegel: "The critical philosophy [of Kant] had, it is true, already turned metaphysics into logic, but it ... was overawed by the object, and so the logical determinations were given an essentially subjective significance with the result that these philosophies remained burdened with the object they avoided and were left with the residue of a thing-in-itself, an infinite obstacle, as a beyond. But the liberation from the opposition of consciousness which the science of logic must be able to presuppose lifts the determinations of thought above this timid, incomplete standpoint and demands that they be considered not with any such limitation and reference but as they are in their own proper character, as logic, as pure reason." *Hegel's Science of Logic*, para. 57.

[16] Hegel, *Hegel's Science of Logic*, p. 197.

[17] Taylor, *Hegel*, p. 49.

non-identity"), Giegerich emphasizes that it is *internal* contraries, and not the clash of two or more independent positions, that the dialectic of interpretation endeavours to fathom. Starting with one thing or one position, the dialectician thinks, not in terms of an external relation of the one to some otherwise independent or extraneous other (though, of course, it can reflect externally related phenomena into themselves when it is the logic of such phenomena that is at issue). Rather, as I have just shown with respect to the trumped-up characterization of Kant's philosophy as having effected a "Copernican revolution," it undermines the naive self-identity of the initial position by discerning self-contradictory dimensions while at the same time thinking in terms of these antinomies of its reason.

Succinctly illustrating this self-contradictory or negativizing moment of the dialectic, Giegerich discussed in his lecture yesterday the phenomenon of willing something. His prime matter in this example was simply the definition of the will as this would be given by traditional logic. Defined in terms of the principle of identity—for which "everything is what it is and not another thing"[18]—the will is nothing else than our human freedom, pure and simple. Just as all bachelors are unmarried men, so the will is synonymous with the idea of freedom. But as Giegerich showed with his example of having the will to complete an advanced degree, the freedom that such willing manifests can require such hard work and sacrifice that we find that we must become a slave insofar as our studies are concerned. Expressing this in a manner that is entirely in keeping with Hegel's formula of the absolute as the identity of identity and difference, Giegerich avers that

> ... to go back to school [for one's Ph.D.] entails the contradiction between my free choice AND my obedience to the 'must' that my choice involves. In willing I am at once free and a slave. The will is the human capacity to be, within oneself, the unity of the unity and difference, of legislating government *and* subject bound by the laws prescribed by this government. For the everyday mind, the will is a unitary thing. That is all. It is simply one of the ultimate constituents of the human psyche. But if you open it up and look into it, you see, as in a clock, its 'moving parts,' its internal 'engine': the inner complexity of the self-contradictory logical life that it is and *as which* it is.

---

[18] Bishop Joseph Butler, cited in D. D. Raphael, *British Moralists 1650-1800*, vol.1 (Indianapolis: Hackett Publishing Co., 1991), preface, para. 384.

DIFFERENT MOMENTS IN DIALECTICAL MOVEMENT

Giegerich's discussion of the slave as the self-contradictory and, therefore, inner other of the idea of willing, may put us in mind of the many inner others we meet with in our dreams. Nowhere is the soulful unity of identity and difference more apparent than in our oneiric productions.[19] Just by "sleeping on it," as we say, the narrowly abstract and self-identical positions of our day dialectically unfold their self-contradictory logical life in an array of strange bedfellows. A student (we may imagine, further to Giegerich's discussion) may actually dream of a slave. Embracing this other as himself (Jung spoke of interpretation of the subjective level), he may find that he is able to get down to work. In subsequent dreams, other figures indicative of further dimensions of the task at hand may appear as well. Immersed in the forest of his research, the student is like a naturalist observing the flora and fauna of some out-of-the-way corner of the world and he dreams of his engagement in these terms.[20] Or again, having completed his preparatory reading, the student dreams of an enormous sailing ship with a vast system of rigging. Recognizing in this ship the other of his ego-identified complaint about feeling "saturated," he finds as well that inspiration quickens within him like a sail unfurling in a powerful wind.[21] And this is to say nothing of the substantial issues of the thesis itself that he may be dialectically grappling with in his dreams at the same time.

Impressed by its multitude of figures, Jung regarded the dream as portraying man as he appears to himself under the aspect of eternity— *sub specie aeternitatis*.[22] Hegel, with much more than only dreams in

---

[19] As useful as it is to appeal to dreams in our attempt to comprehend the self-contradictory unfolding of the one as an array of inner others, it is important to realize that the interiority that the dialectic constitutes is not the *positive* interiority of the dream world or even of "the unconscious." While dreams, to be sure, do image something of the dialectical movement to which we give the name soul, the interiority of the soul is the mediate interiority or inwardness of anything at all, not only of the complexes and dream figures that we suppose to be inside us. As Giegerich has pointed out, dream images, inasmuch as we simply perceive them in their sensuous immediacy as they appear in front of our observing consciousness, are as external as things. The corollary of this is also true. When perceived in terms of the inner community that the dialectic unfolds, the so-called external world is interiorized into itself, which is also to say, subjectively or psychologically realized.

[20] The words "is like" in this sentence think the unity of identity and difference.

[21] With the image of a sail unfurling in the wind, we have once again an image figurative of that essence of the will, freedom. Though this moment would properly belong to our next section, which will be concerned with the negation of the negation, such is the power of the dialectic that we cannot help but get ahead of ourselves here.

[22] Jung, *CW* 8 § 316.

mind, spoke in a similar vein of mediation and inner infinity. Mimetic to dreams, the self-contradictory unfolding of any prime matter into the figures that are its others, mediates the fullness of that matter even as it embeds what would otherwise be merely an abstraction (i.e., an identity without the difference that is its other) in the plenum of its real and existing context. As Hegel expresses this, "The true is thus the bacchanalian whirl in which no member is not drunken; and because each, as soon as it detaches itself, dissolves immediately—the whirl is just as much transparent and simple repose."[23]

Before turning to the next moment in the dialectic, I want to share with you briefly a number of quotations from authors of importance to the tradition of depth psychology that are pertinent to the ideas we have touched upon in this section.

The first is a passage from Samuel Taylor Coleridge, the poet-philosopher who can be credited with having coined the term "psychoanalysis" almost a century before Freud. Reasoning with reference to what he variously calls the Sum, I am, spirit, self, and self-consciousness, Coleridge writes,

> ... it is a subject which becomes a subject by the act of constructing itself objectively to itself; but which never is an object except for itself, and only so far as by the very same act it becomes a subject. It may be described therefore as a perpetual self-duplication of one and the same power into object and subject, which presuppose each other, and can exist only as antitheses.[24]

A second amplification comes from Jung. Writing in a similar vein to Coleridge, the psychologist states that "... *in religious experience man comes face to face with a psychically overwhelming Other.*" A few lines later he continues, "Only something overwhelming, no matter what form of expression it uses, can challenge the whole man and force him to react as a whole."[25] Clearly, the other referred to here, inasmuch as it compels man to act as a whole, is man's own other, his inner other. And this is so, it is important to add, even when its form of expression is that of an empirically existing external other. As the unity of identity

---

[23] Cited by Taylor in *Hegel*, pp. 107-108.
[24] Samuel Taylor Coleridge, *Biographia Literaria*, 2 vols. (1817) (Princeton: Princeton University Press, 1983), 1: 268.
[25] Jung, *CW* 10 § 655.

and difference, an inclusive thinking-it-all-a-once mode of thought, dialectics overcomes the distinction between external and internal. Inverting this relation, interiority, as constituted by the dialectic, is no longer inside or surrounded by the outwardness of things. Indeed, it could even be said that the outward is no more. For by reflecting everything external into itself (which is also to say, by adumbrating the self-contradictions that belie the self-identical identity of each position or thing), the dialectic inaugurates an absolute form of interiority or soulful intensity.

Several further passages from Jung spring to mind. Writing with respect to the psychology of the transference, Jung states:

> The unrelated human being lacks wholeness, for he can achieve wholeness only through the soul, and the soul cannot exist without its other side, which is always found in a "You." Wholeness is a combination of I and You, and these show themselves to be parts of a transcendent unity whose nature can only be grasped symbolically ....[26]

That it is not an external relationship that is being spoken of here, but an internal relation that has unfolded itself through an external one or as an external one is brought out in Jung's subsequent sentences:

> The alchemists even go so far as to say that the *corpus, anima,* and *spiritus* of the arcane substance are one, "because they are all from the One, and of the One, and with the One, which is the root of itself."[27]

Relating this to the transference's "alluring sexual aspect," which "is always trying to deliver us into the power of a partner who seems compounded of all the qualities we have failed to realize in ourselves," Jung writes in another section of the same work:

> Hence, unless we prefer to be made fools of by our illusions, we shall, by carefully analyzing every fascination, extract from it a portion of our own personality, like a quintessence, and slowly come to recognize that we meet ourselves time and again in a thousand disguises on the paths of life.[28]

---

[26] Jung, *CW* 16, § 454.
[27] *Ibid.*
[28] *Ibid.*, § 534.

Jung's insight here—that we repeatedly meet ourselves in others—applies as well to remote, cross-cultural figures. In descriptions of that figure of the other that he called the anima, Jung describes this archetypal figure as often appearing in the form of a woman from another culture or from an earlier historical epoch.[29] Similarly, in a sentence that can be read as an allusion to his notion of the collective unconscious, Jung avers that our "growing familiarity with the spirit of the East should be taken merely as a sign that we are beginning to relate to alien elements within ourselves."[30] Surely there is resonance here with Hegel's idea of the identity of identity and difference.

Let us stay with Jung a little longer. The dialectical unfolding of the one into the others that present the different moments of its truth is brought about, as we discussed above, through the self-contradiction or negation of the naively self-identical starting point. Capturing something of this dialectical movement in a felicitous phrase, Jung writes, "the individual may strive after perfection ... but must suffer from the opposite of his intentions for the sake of his completeness."[31] In Jung's terminology, the dynamic here is one of compensation. The unconscious, for Jung, stands in a compensatory relation to consciousness. When the conscious attitude is too narrowly self-identical, or as Jung would say, too one-sided, it is compensatorily thwarted, contradicted, and negated by the others that it creates round itself if only by having excluded them. "And though I deny it a thousand times," writes Jung of "the unexpectedly dark Brother" which the Christian West encounters in other faiths, "*it is also in me.*"[32] And so it is that the biblical story places the Magi from the East by the manger of Christ's nativity. The absolute truly is the unity of identity and difference, individual and universal, stable and star.

The notions we have been discussing in this section—self-contradiction, negation, the unity of identity and difference, inner infinity, and the bacchanalian whirl—deepen our understanding, not only of dreams and transferences, but of symptoms, too. Our symptoms are at once the self-contradictory, negativizing agents

---

[29] Jung, *CW* 9, i § 518; *CW* 10 § 714; *CW* 12 § 112.
[30] Jung, *CW* 13 § 72.
[31] Jung, *CW* 9, ii § 123.
[32] Jung, *CW* 18 § 1472.

through which the soul transforms itself and the soul's presentation of itself to itself as its own other.

Speaking with reference to the symptom as the starting point of psychoanalysis, Freud characterizes it as "a thing that is more foreign to the ego than anything else in the mind."[33] Jung, for his part, has much the same view. It is Hillman, however, with his notion of "pathologizing" that makes the most of the dialectical unfolding, or "falling apart" as he calls it, of the one into many via symptom formation. In keeping with what we have been calling the negativizing action of self-contradiction, Hillman defines pathologizing as "the psyche's autonomous ability to create illness, morbidity, disorder, abnormality, and suffering in any aspect of its behaviour, and to experience and imagine life through this deformed and afflicted perspective."[34] Like the stage of the alchemical opus known as the *putrefactio* or *mortificatio*, pathologizing is a transforming corruption or going under of the naive A = A self-identical starting point.

Our dreams, transferences, and symptoms are to the Hegelian point: The exegesis of the one is dialectically revelatory of the one's internal other(s). In and through the various self-contradictions that arise in these and other phenomena, the prime matter presents itself to itself as an other or as a series of others.[35]

Negation of the Negation

In *Thus Spoke Zarathustra*, Nietzsche's other, the dialectician and sage Zarathustra, declares: "Always once one—in the long run that makes two."[36] Cited in the present context, this adage succinctly captures the essence of what we have been discussing thus far, i.e., the dialectical

---

[33] Sigmund Freud, *New Introductory Lectures on Psycho-Analysis*, tr. W. J. H. Sprott (London: Hogarth Press, 1933), p. 78.

[34] James Hillman, "On the Necessity of Abnormal Psychology: Ananke and Athene," *Facing the Gods*, ed. J. Hillman (Irving, Texas: Spring Publications, 1980), p. 1.

[35] An analogy can be drawn here to the traditional Eskimos living off the land in the arctic. Knowing snow from within, the Eskimos had a great many names for the substance, as many as there were moments of its truth to be known. Likewise, the dialectician thinkingly enters the hermeneutical 'tundra' of whatever the matter at hand may be, the better to generate the rationally necessary (and at the same time, existentially crucial) distinctions by which it is known from within in the various moments of its truth.

[36] Friedrich Nietzsche, *Thus Spoke Zarathustra*, tr. R. J. Hollingdale (Harmondsworth: Penguin Books, 1961), p. 82.

unfolding of an initial proposition or starting point in terms of its non-identical or self-contradictory other(s).

Also called the simple or first negation, this dialectical unfolding of the one into two is a most familiar experience. In the idiom of the present age it is good-humouredly known as "Murphy's Law." Recognizing the work of the negative through our lives, this colloquialism simply states that "if anything can go wrong, it will go wrong."

Now our task in this section is to elucidate the movement beyond the simple negation, so aptly summed up in Murphy's Law, to what in the dialectics of Hegel is called the negation of the negation. But first let us linger a while longer with what is known as the simple negation. Though this moment of the dialectic was the topic of the previous section, it is crucial to get a sure grasp of it before undertaking to discuss its subsequent—or when thought is in full flight, simultaneous—negation.

Briefly summarizing, we can say that initial consciousness, in its naiveté, claims to know the world, or the feature of it that is at issue, *immediately*, or as Giegerich often puts this, *"just like that."* However, reflecting at best a partial truth, this position soon falls foul of its own trajectory inasmuch as what it has asserted as its reach can be shown to be contradicted by its actually more limited grasp. Anomalies emerge, loose ends appear, symptoms afflict. Recalling our earlier discussion of Kant, we can add that in cases where the initial position has had the form of a synthetic judgment, this judgment is cancelled by another that has the opposite meaning. Since, when measured against themselves in the other, both accounts cannot be true at the same time (consciousness being unable yet to think the unity of identity and difference), certainty is negated.

Now let us add some colour to our account of this simple, first-level sense of negation. Beset by contradiction, consciousness may react by drawing the wagon train into a circle, the better to keep the Indians out! Or shaken in its A = A type certainty, it may obsessively review its holdings, in the manner of the miserly Scrooge, to make sure that nothing is missing, nothing lost. Jung speaks in this connection of a "conservative adherence to the earlier attitude."[37] Alternatively, or in the aftermath of the above-mentioned resistances having failed,

---

[37] Jung, *CW* 4 § 350.

consciousness may accept the negation, if only in a manner that is still indicative of the immediate-mindedness of its former mode of knowing. Drawing upon a term used by Aristotle, Jung speaks of this dynamic as an *enantiodromia*. Reversing itself (we may think here of the undoing of the tragic hero), consciousness simply turns around to the opposite view to what it had previously held. Where before it had been characterized by a self-identical certainty, now it has become just as self-identically *un*certain. The picture here is one of the dry sceptic, the bitter cynic, or more transparently still, of the adamant ex-believer, the one who is now as fundamentalistic in his atheism as he had formerly been in his theism.

Horror upon contradiction, heads accumulate? We might wonder, rather, if the guillotine of negativity has even chopped a single one! Unable to sustain its initial claim that A is identical to A and all is right with the world, and hoping to stay well back of the cutting edge it has discovered in its own brain, consciousness readily identifies itself with the threatening counter-proposition that A does not equal A and that all is not right with the world. This apparent forfeiture of the former identity-based vision, however, can hardly be called a real grappling with difference. A defence against difference (Anna Freud spoke of "identification with the aggressor"), it is rather more like a down-sizing of the initial claim. Stoically withdrawing itself from the difference it seems to admit, and sometimes even taking up spiritual exercises to maintain its equanimity in the face of its doppelgängering other, consciousness surreptitiously holds on to the principle of identity, if only in the form of what could be described as an agoraphobic self-sameness.

Let us examine this a little closer still. Having pushed off by means of the first negation from the "just-like-that" mode that had formerly identified it with its contents, consciousness has begun, if only minimally, to come home to itself as negativity, self-consciousness, reflectivity, and doubt. This reflective negativity and doubt-filled self-consciousness, however, is still only the reverse of the former positive stance. As such, the position it now stands for is dependent upon the mediation which the position it has come to disavow continues to provide, if only through its being disavowed. This is a contradiction. No more than Scrooge could dispel with invective humbug the ghosts that visited him on Christmas Eve can the first negation dispel the positions—past, present and future—as which the work of the negative continues. Nor can the little death that the first negation had brought give consciousness the right to claim, with immediate Shakespearean licence, that "Death once dead, there's no more dying then."[38] Just as one poem does not a poet make, so it takes not one negation but many for consciousness to become as at home in its other as it is in itself.

We may now turn more directly to the subject of this section, the negation of the negation. In *The Soul's Logical Life*, as in his lecture to us yesterday, Giegerich makes the subtle, yet important point that the negation of the negation is a quieter process than the dramatic clash that brings about a first negation.[39] Taking this point into consideration, we may be reminded, by way of contrast, of the much noisier accounts Jung gives of what he called the compensatory relationship of the conscious and unconscious. As described by Jung, the compensations which the unconscious metes out are often thunderously loud. Speaking of this in religious terms, he presents the idea that God can be known in whatever it is that upsets or overwhelms us—in an affect, perhaps, or some event that befalls us, whether this be from within or without: "Time out of mind [God] has been the psychically stronger, capable of throwing your conscious purposes off the rails, fatally thwarting them and occasionally making mincemeat of them."[40] Now there is no doubt that compensations of the kind Jung here describes occur, or that on the "road to individuation" the ego will have to take its share of beatings. The "experience of the self," writes Jung, "is always a defeat for the ego."[41] The point that must be grasped in this seminar, however (and in grasping this we begin to see the movement Giegerich has taken beyond Jung), is that even a million compensations cannot produce the negation of the negation, for while seeming to embrace its negation in the compensation which it receives from the Self, the ego continues to preserve its ultimate concerns from negation by projecting them beyond itself as its idealized other, *its* Self.

---

[38] Sonnet 146, l. 14.
[39] Wolfgang Giegerich, *The Soul's Logical Life: Towards a Rigorous Notion of Psychology* (Frankfurt am Main, Peter Lang GmbH, 1998), p. 200.
[40] C. G. Jung, *Letters*, vol. 2: *1951-1961*, ed. G. Adler and A. Jaffe, trans. R. F. C. Hull (Princeton: Princeton University Press, 1975), pp. 4-5.
[41] Jung, *CW* 14: 778. Italics in original.

In its so-called defeat the most it can say is *mea culpa*, I'm to blame. I, as a fallible human being, have failed to be a good Christian or analyst or whatever. In saying this, however, consciousness preserves its god-term from critique.[42]

A distinction may be helpful here. In his writings, Giegerich frequently distinguishes between the "semantic" or content level of consciousness and the "syntactic" level of its overall structure or form. Change at the semantic level merely involves a shifting around of the contents of consciousness in the light of their having been contradicted it some way. This shifting around, however, as extensive as it may be in many cases, poses no challenge to the *form* of consciousness. None of its contents, that is to say, has yet become the straw that breaks the camel's back. In the negation of the negation, by contrast, the camel's back is broken, the structure of consciousness torn asunder.

Now let us slip the word "theology" in here as a synonym for consciousness at the syntactic level. Theologically figured, the statement, "I ... [have] seen tribulation by the rod of His wrath,"[43] aptly characterizes that moment of the dialectic we have been calling the simple negation. In this scenario the ego is turned from its partial views and illusions as it suffers what Jung calls the violence that is done to it by the Self. The negation of the negation, however, happens on a whole different plane. Rather than being something that happens to us within our individuation process and theology, making us cry out or gnash our teeth, it is quietly, and yet more radically, a process that is undergone by our theology, i.e., it is a logical negation. "We are actually living in the time of the splitting of the world and the invalidation of Christ," writes Jung, touching on this more radical negation in a letter to Fr. Victor White.[44]

More like a dying God than an ego that has known the wrath of unconscious compensation, consciousness begins to slip from its A = A ("I am that I am"!) throne of certainty and to go under. Portraying this moment of syntactic collapse in the figure of Apollo calling out to Mnemosyne as he dies, Keats writes:

---

[42] For an in-depth discussion of the *mea culpa* position see Wolfgang Giegerich, "The Advent of the Guest: Shadow Integration and the Rise of Psychology," *Spring 51: A Journal of Archetype and Culture* (Dallas: Spring Publications, 1991), pp.100-102.

[43] Lamentations 3:1.

[44] Jung, *Letters*, vol. 2, p. 138.

> Soon wild commotions shook him, and made flush
> All the immortal fairness of his limbs;
> Most like the struggle at the gate of death;
> Or liker still to one who should take leave
> Of pale immortal death, and with a pang
> As hot as death's is chill, with fierce convulse
> Die into life ....[45]

True to the moment of the dialectic we are attempting to elucidate here, the first negation, which Keats says is "like the struggle at the gate of death," is followed by a second that is "liker still to one who should take leave of pale immortal death." That this 'taking leave of' or 'pushing off from' the first negation is indeed the work of a second-order negation is evident in the sublation that it yields in the final phrase: "Die into life ...."

Now, of course, the mere mention of a dying God calls to mind Nietzsche's declaration of the death of God. This, it might be thought, is figurative of the negation of the negation. Giegerich's comment regarding the *quietness* of the sublating, second-order negation, however, helps us to discern that such is not the case. The negation of the negation has an entirely different feeling-tone than the one that comes across from the philosopher's spectacular announcement. Alluding to Kleinian categories, we can say that in contrast to Nietzsche's paranoidly triumphant tone, the negation of the negation is more depressive and sad. Far from becoming some Nietzschean overman, consciousness is humbled to know itself as the unity of the identity and difference of human and divine.[46]

Drawing upon alchemical metaphors, Giegerich likens the negation of the negation to those phases of the opus in which transformation takes place via fermenting putrefaction and internal corruption. Recognizing itself in its contradictory other, consciousness comes to the painful realization that it has protested its initial position too loudly. With this realization it becomes an "unhappy consciousness," as Hegel puts it. Cringing at the thought of its former righteousness and naïveté, it starts

---

[45] John Keats, "Hyperion: A Fragment," Bk. III, lines 124-130.
[46] Here, with this reference to the humbling recognition of the identity and difference of human and divine, I have in mind James Hillman's notion of "Dehumanizing or Soul-Making." See the chapter with this title in his *Re-Visioning Psychology* (New York: Harper & Row, 1975).

to collapse from within and to go under. Its shame, however, is a higher shame, the beginning of its sublation.[47]

Two pictorial representations come to my mind at this juncture as being illustrative of this moment of sublating collapse. One is from a dream that I heard many years ago; the other from a Greek myth.

In the dream, the figure of the dreamer tells his sister in a very authoritative manner about the phases of the moon. The sister, however, is not convinced by his account. Irritated by this, the figure of the dreamer reiterates what he has said in a more exactingly pedantic, even bullying, manner. This happens several times, until finally the sister accedes to his account, *at which point another moon appears!* Along with this second, contradictory moon comes the sense that even further moons could appear, perhaps even an infinite number. The impact of this upon the dream-ego is considerable. Suffice it to say, he has no more lessons to give. While the first negation—i.e., his sister's doubts about what he was telling her—had only inspired him to give a more detailed account, the appearance of the second moon was truly humbling in that it forced the figure of the dreamer to admit that the cosmic syntax of the night sky was no longer what he had so knowingly claimed it to be.[48]

The Greek myth that has also come to my mind in relation to the negation of the negation is the tale of Pentheus's dismemberment. As lacking in what Keats called "negative capability"[49] as was the figure of the dreamer in the dream we just discussed, consciousness in the figure of Pentheus, a king of Thebes, resists the introduction of the worship of Bacchus into his Kingdom. This resistance, however, soon becomes the opposite of itself. Dialectically affronted by contradictions, Pentheus discovers that the women of his kingdom, his mother Agave and her sisters among them, have left their domestic duties to join the revel-rout of the god. With the aim of following after the women and spying on them, the king, at Bacchus's prompting, disguises himself as a woman. No sooner has he donned the garb of

---

[47] For a discussion of "higher shame" see my "Slinking Towards Bethlehem: A Prospective View of Shame," *Spring 67: A Journal of Archetype and Culture* (Woodstock, CT: Spring Journal, 2000), pp. 19-37.

[48] For a different discussion of this dream see my *The Dove in the Consulting Room: Hysteria and the Anima in Bollas and Jung* (Hove: Brunner-Routledge, 2003), p. 102.

[49] John Keats, *Selected Poems and Letters*, ed. D. Bush (Boston: Houghton Mifflin, 1959), p. 261.

the maenads, however, than the madness of the god overtakes him and he begins to see double. Looking at the sun (even as the dream-ego in our dream had looked at the moon) he sees not one fiery orb, but two. The same doubling occurs with respect to his city, Thebes, and to the parts of his own body. Identical with themselves, these are, at the same time, beside themselves, that is, logically different if still perceptually self-same. When Pentheus subsequently finds the women, this identity-dissembling, doubling movement becomes absolute. While watching the cavorting women from a treetop, the king is spotted by his mother. Seeing her son as his other (that is, as Bacchus in animal form), the frenzied Agave drags him down from his perch and tears him limb from limb with the aid of the other maenads.

I think that it is very likely that Hegel was alluding to this initiatory ritual of dismemberment, famously portrayed by Euripides in *The Bacchantes*, when he spoke, in the passage cited earlier, of truth as "the bacchanalian whirl in which no member is not drunken." Indeed, the second part of this passage—"and because each, as soon as it detaches itself, dissolves immediately ..."—seems to point directly to the detached Pentheus watching from his treetop. Encountering this motif the *consensus Jungian* has often given it a weak and moralistic reading, as for instance when it has regarded the dismemberment of Pentheus as the fate which the patriarchal ego has prepared for itself through its neglect of the feminine.[50] Hegel's concluding phrase, however, suggests a more dialectical reading. Thinking the unity of identity (Pentheus) and difference (Bacchus and the maenads), Hegel avers that "the whirl is just as much transparent and simple repose" as it is bacchanalian orgy or whirl. Transposing this formula into the figurative terms of the myth, we could say with Giegerich that Pentheus, Bacchus, Agave, and the rest are sublated moments of the one idea which the myth unfolds. Just as psychology is the unity of *psyche* and *logos*, so a psychological reading of myth thinks the syzygy of soul and spirit even as it follows "the 'analytic' unfolding, in pictorial form, of the internal complexities, the living dialectic, of the standpoint of psychology."[51]

---

[50] Cf. Wolfgang Giegerich, "The 'Patriarchal Neglect of the Feminine Principle': A Psychological Fallacy in Jungian Theory," in *Harvest: Journal for Jungian Studies*, 45.1 (1999): 7-30.

[51] Wolfgang Giegerich, "'Different Moments of Truth'—A Few Examples," in this volume, p. 26.

Another line from Hegel helps us to a more dialectical understanding of the Pentheus story. Cited by Giegerich in the text of his first lecture, this line is as follows: "But the life of the Spirit is not the life that shrinks from death and keeps itself untouched by devastation, but rather the life that endures it and maintains itself in it."[52] While seeming to shrink from the death that comes to him in the form of Bacchus and the maenads, Pentheus does not keep himself untouched by devastation. As much Bacchus's other as Bacchus is his, he endures contradiction and maintains himself in it. It would not be enough for one of these opposed figures to simply prevail, for Pentheus, say, to simply become a satyr and enter the retinue of the god. For as we have already heard from Hegel, "... neither of these determinations, taken alone, has truth; this belongs only to their unity."[53] A sublated moment in that unity of identity and difference by which truth is constituted, Pentheus's resistance of the bacchanalian whirl is, at the same time as it is that, his susceptibility to its devastation and his maintaining himself through this. Initiatory dismemberment—the negation of the negation—cannot be accomplished without this resolve of the subject to maintain itself through death. To think dialectically, we must be as stringently rigorous and narrow-minded as we are imaginative and broad-minded—both Penthean and maenadic at once.

A few more lines from Hegel are apt in relation to the myth we have been discussing. Following immediately upon the line we quoted above about the life of the spirit maintaining itself through death, the philosopher continues:

> It [the life of the spirit] wins its truth only when, in utter dismemberment, it finds itself. It is this power, not as something positive, which closes its eyes to the negative as when we say of something that it is nothing or is false, and then having done with it, turn away and pass on to something else; on the contrary, spirit is this power only by looking the negative in the face, and tarrying with it. This tarrying with the negative is the magical power that converts it into being.[54]

---

[52] G. W. F. Hegel, *Phenomenology of Spirit*, tr. A. V. Miller (Oxford: Oxford University Press, 1977), p. 19.
[53] Hegel, *Hegel's Science of Logic*, p. 197.
[54] Hegel, *Phenomenology of the Spirit*, p. 19.

Absolute Negative Interiorization

We come now to the final moment of the dialectic, that of absolute negative interiorization. Absolute negative interiorization is the thinking-all-at-once of the previous moments we have discussed. This thinking-all-at-once, however, should not be thought of as the culminating moment that is produced in sequence or series from the other three. While pictorially we do represent it in this manner, it may now be understood that the dialectic thinks the all-at-onceness of its various moments from the outset as already sublated moments of itself. But, of course, this thinking-it-all-at-once-from-the-outset is only implicit and must be unfolded, as we have attempted to do in adumbrating its various moments above.

A passage from Jung's writings may help to make this clearer. In his "Foreword to Suzuki's *Introduction to Zen Buddhism*," Jung defines the unconscious as "an irrepresentable totality of all sublimated psychic factors, a 'total vision' *in potentia*." This "'total vision' *in potentia*," he then adds, "constitutes the total disposition from which consciousness singles out tiny fragments from time to time."[55] Now it must be immediately pointed out that there is a contradiction here: *total* vision is, at the same time as it is that, an *irrepresentable* vision. In seeing *everything* (i.e., a situation or image in all of its complexity, all of its moments) it *sees* nothing. This contradiction, however, is a dialectical one, or, rather, it would be that except for the fact that Jung holds it back from being fully so through his still positivized distinction between consciousness and the unconscious. But pushing off with Giegerich from this distinction, we easily know what Jung means. Total vision is not representable; it is not vision at all, but sublated vision, thought. Putting this another way, we can say that for vision to be total it has to be *absolute* vision, that is, vision that has been *absolved* from the differences that make sensory impressions or imaginal images distinct and different from one another. Such "vision," however, is not a "picturing" any more; it is neither immediate sense certainty nor the first negation of this, the imagining mode of sensory intuition. And yet, going back on this a bit (even as the brothers in yesterday's fairy tale slipped back on the mountain slope), it can be said that on its way home to itself absolute negativity or "the soul" can indeed appear to itself in the

---

[55] Jung, *CW* 11 § 897.

aspect of a contingent figure, that is, as something particular, singular, and finite even as, in Jung's words, "tiny fragments," expressive of the "total disposition," are "single[d] out ... from time to time." As Giegerich has written, " ... in the idea of [the *psyche* as] self-relation ... otherness ... is not totally lost ..., it is inherent in it as a sublated moment, inasmuch as the self that does the reflecting and the self that is being reflected are both identical and different."[56] But this said, we must also understand that the soul's true homecoming resides in the further distillation, vaporization or interiorization of this figuration of itself as other into the logical form of consciousness itself. Again, to quote Giegerich, "What at first appears as a content of consciousness is in truth the seed of what wants to become a new form of consciousness at large."[57]

Now, reviewing what I have just written, I find myself thinking of Jung's description of himself as having, as he once put it, had "to climb down a thousand ladders until I could reach out my hand to the little clod of earth that I am."[58] Evidently, my account of Jung's notion of "total vision" still has a few ladders to come down if the ground upon which Giegerich has positioned himself is to be reached. Taking this step, we must understand that when the aforementioned "seed of what wants to become a new form of consciousness" has done so, Jung's "tiny fragment" (whatever that may be in any particular case) is no longer the numinous image or symbol that the implicitness of thought (= Jung's "'total vision' *in potentia*") had previously out-pictured its potential to become explicit as. Rather, having actualized itself as conceptual comprehension through the particular phenomenon at hand (which, as its other, it has hermeneutically entered and uroborically filled[59]), it now *knows* that phenomenon (prime matter, tiny fragment, situation, issue, image, etc.) in *its* totality or *as* totality. Little clod of earth that I am indeed!

---

[56] Wolfgang Giegerich, "Is the Soul 'Deep'? Entering and Following the Logical Movement of Heraclitus' 'Fragment 45.'" *Spring 64: A Journal of Archetype and Culture* (Woodstock, CT: Spring Journal, 1998), p. 11.
[57] Giegerich, "Is the Soul 'Deep'?" p. 19.
[58] Jung, *Letters, vol. 2*, p. 19, no. 8.
[59] Taylor writes in *Hegel*, p. 129: "[Hegel's] aim is simply to follow the movement in his object of study. The task of the philosopher 'is to submerge his freedom in [the content], and let it be moved by its own nature.' If the argument follows a dialectical movement, then this must be in the things themselves, not just in the way we reason about them."

Above I referred to Giegerich's point about the quietness of the negation of the negation. When carried forward, this analogy can also be used to convey what is meant by absolute-negative interiorization. Consider, for example, the foundation-voiding speculativity of the 'music' that sounds, absolute-negatively, through the quietness of Keats' line, "heard melodies are sweet, but those unheard are sweeter."[60] And further to this, there is Wordsworth's famous definition of poetry as "emotion recollected in tranquility."[61]

It might be assumed that we are speaking of the numinous here. As a Jungian analyst I have learned to use the words "numinous" and "numinosity" with respect to what Jung called "*a priori* emotional value."[62] Images, too, inasmuch as they are as Jung describes them— tiny fragments singled out from the psyche's total vision—I have regarded as numinous. Absolute negativity, however, like the melody that is the sweeter for being unheard and the emotion that becomes poetry by being recollected in tranquility, is the numinosity that these both have, not in the positivity of their having it as such,

---

[60] John Keats, "Ode on a Grecian Urn," lines 11-12. The verse continues: " … therefore, ye soft pipes, play on; / Not to the sensual ear, but, more endear'd, / Pipe to the spirit ditties of no tone …."

[61] Returned to its actual context in paragraph 26 of Wordsworth's "Preface of the *Lyrical Ballads*, this line has rather the opposite meaning to that which my citation of it here implies. In Wordsworth's view, "… emotion is contemplated till, by a species of reaction, the tranquility gradually disappears, and an emotion, kindred to that which was before the subject of contemplation, is gradually produced, and does itself actually exist in the mind." Now in taking care to note Wordsworth's actual and different meaning, we may come to a more dialectical understanding of what I have variously referred to as "quiet," "recollection," and "tranquility." These terms, as I refer to them, can also reach a crescendo, not of emotion or aesthetic image (though these, to be sure, remain present as sublated moments), but out of the intensiveness of the reflection of emotion and image into themselves, that is, into the thought that they implicitly are. Pushing off then from Wordsworth's rather literal account of emotion recollected in tranquility to Giegerich's negatively interiorized view, the following passage is most pertinent. Critiquing the positivized spatial image of the soul as deep, Giegerich argues that this idea wards off the corrupting, fermenting power of the soul's internal dynamic "by depriving it of its logical, notional, intellectual claims and challenge and instead translating it into the harmlessness and fuzziness of a mere romantic feeling." Recollecting emotion in tranquility at a whole different level than was possible for Wordsworth, he continues: "Emotions, feelings, are an excellent packaging for safely storing the logical or 'metaphysical' dynamite of contents away. If you construe a conflict as an emotion or feeling, you have successfully removed it from the battlefield of truth and reduced it to the banal level of personal, subjective, or interpersonal problems" ["Is the Soul 'Deep'?," p. 19]. There is crescendo in this passage, not the noisy one of "personal, subjective, or interpersonal problems," but of the "metaphysical dynamite" or "fermenting corruption" that logical movement brings.

[62] Jung, *CW* 6 § 791.

but as recollected in the quiet of Mnemosyne, that is, as knowing consciousness, the life of the mind, logical movement, thought. In is the presence of these powerful, and yet intangible, realities that absolute negativity establishes and affirms.

True Psychology

In his "Foreword" to *Hegel's Logic*, J. N. Findlay sums up the essence of the dialectical approach:

> The action of thought is to *negate* the basis from which it starts, to show it up as not being self-subsistent, and so to have in it a springboard from which it can ascend to what is truly self-subsistent and self-explanatory.[63]

Reflecting upon this passage, we may be put in mind of the springboard of negation through which psychoanalysis pushed off from its earliest form of itself to become a self-subsisting discipline in its own right. I refer, of course, to Freud's rejection—we could also say, negation—of the seduction theory. Believing, prior to 1897, that the hysterical patients he had been treating could be understood in the light of their having been sexually traumatized by an adult pervert during childhood, Freud came, after that date, to realize that such a theoretical view was contradictory. There were just too many patients suffering from hysteria for the conclusion that they had all been sexually abused to be sustained. While, doubtless, some patients had been abused (Freud did not "abandon" the seduction theory, but rather, retained it as a sublated possibility under the wider theory that was to follow), the prospect that all had been could be maintained only if fatherhood were thoroughly demonized. Springing free from this negated positive basis in the seduction theory, Freud wrote in an 1898 letter to Fliess, "… initially I had defined the etiology [of hysteria] too narrowly; the share of fantasy in it is far greater than I thought in the beginning."[64] This sentence contains an important insight. Or more

---

[63] John N. Findlay, "Foreword," G. W. F. Hegel, *Hegel's Logic: Being Part One of the Encyclopedia of Philosophical Sciences* (1830), tr. William Wallace (Oxford: Clarendon Press/OUP, 1975), p. xii.

[64] Sigmund Freud, *The Complete Letters of Sigmund Freud to Wilhelm Fliess: 1887-1904*, ed. & tr. Jeffery M. Masson (London: The Belknap Press of Harvard University Press, 1985), p. 311.

than that, as a decisive pushing off from positivity and the external into the inwardness of fantasy and reflection, it conveys that an essential shift in how insight in general is to be conceived has occurred. Now for Freud to get to this, for him to "no longer believe in [his] *neurotica*,"[65] he had had to allow the syntax of that theory to be 'dragged through the knot-hole backwards,' as it were, of the very clinical material he had assembled as evidence for it. Said another way, the fantasy material that his consciousness, in the form of the seduction theory, had taken too literally to heart became the "seed," as Giegerich put it in a passage quoted earlier, of what became "a new form of consciousness at large,"[66] a new theory. Fantasy, not fact, he now held to be the decisive etiological factor in the neuroses. Of course, this change in the constitution of psychology was reflected in the mirror of its other as something happening within the patients. Exactly paralleling the seduction theory's having gone under via an *internal* corruption into Freud's new view, the patients in this new view were regarded as suffering, not from external corruption due to seduction by the father, but from internal corruption, that is, from their own fantasies and wishes pertaining to seducing and being seduced.

Freud, however, no sooner ascended to this more logically negative view than he externalized and positivized it again in his theory of infantile sexuality, and later, of the Oedipus complex. With this development, the patients' dreams and fantasies were taken to be *representative* of something more biological-factual—sex and the family—and a vast edifice of knowledge was built up about these subjects. Now, the critical point here is not that these fields of inquiry are unimportant. Rather, it is that Freud, by finding in them a positive base for his psychology project, failed to comprehend what Giegerich calls "the psychological difference."[67]

Referring back to the quote from Findlay at the top of this section, let us recall that "the action of thought is to *negate* the basis from which it starts." Likewise, the "psychological difference" from which a truly *psychological* psychology springs resides in the recognition that psychology, in the strict sense of that term, is not about anything positive—not childhood, sexuality, the family, gender issues, people and their problems,

---

[65] Freud, *Complete Letters of Sigmund Freud to Wilhelm Fliess*, p. 265.
[66] *Ibid.*, p. 19.
[67] Giegerich, *The Soul's Logical Life*, p. 123-124.

dreams and fantasies, etc. Rather, it is about the *logical form* through which such phenomena are reflected into themselves in the course of our recognizing, not just once as in 1897, but again and again, that the action of thought is to negate its own base.

Psychology, for Giegerich, is reflection into itself; it is about the bottomlessness of its own ever-negated base, absolute negativity, "the soul." As regards the usual suspects—the above mentioned subjects that do not in their positivity constitute psychology (childhood, sexuality, people's problems, dreams, etc.)—psychology, it may be said, is as the reflection of these into themselves. In individual analysis, for example, the stories told in the history, the domestic issues presented, the childhood memories recalled, the dreams, and all and sundry are listened to in much the same way as Dr. Giegerich worked with the fairy tale and myths in his lectures yesterday, that is, as already interiorized unities of identity and difference, statements of "the soul" regarding itself. Interrogating whatever starting point it takes in the light of the contradictions inherent in it (which is also to say, by thinking across the associations and topic changes the unity of their identity and difference), "psychology begins where any phenomenon (whether physical or mental, 'real' or fantasy image) is interiorized absolute-negatively into itself, and I find myself in its inner infinity. This is what it takes; psychology cannot be had for less."[68]

Giegerich's reference in the previous sentence to what it takes to have psychology (we could also say, to the price that must be paid to have a true psychology) brings to mind Freud's well-known contrast between what he called "the copper of ... suggestion" and the "pure gold of analysis." We might assume from this distinction of Freud's that he would have concurred with Giegerich's insistence that "psychology cannot be had for less." However, when we look at the actual passage in which Freud uses these expressions we find, on the contrary, that he is offering to peddle the wares of his psychoanalysis at discount prices!

> It is very probable, too, that the application of our therapy to numbers [to greater numbers of people] will compel us to alloy the pure gold of analysis plentifully with the copper of direct suggestion; and hypnotic influence might find a place

---

[68] Giegerich, "Is the Soul 'Deep'?" p. 31.

> in it again, too. ... But whatever form this therapy for the people may take, whatever the elements out of which it must be compounded, its most effective and most important ingredients will assuredly remain those borrowed from strict psycho-analysis which serves no ulterior purpose.[69]

This is an odd and contradictory passage. In the last line, Freud piously refers to the "strict psycho-analysis which serves no ulterior purpose." The whole context in which this line occurs, however, is fraught with ulterior purpose. With the aim of disseminating its positivized findings and promoting itself in the world, psychoanalysis will act out all that it strictly forbids itself within its own austere confines in the form of a therapy for the people. Now, the problem with this is not that the large number of people needing therapy should not have the benefit of it. As far as psychotherapy is concerned, the more down-to-earth the better, I say. Nor is it, as some would wish, that analysis should be kept identical with itself and pure. The problem, rather, resides in the taking prisoner of every thought that the people have for the furtherance of the issues that psychoanalysis—Freudian, Jungian or of whatever stripe—holds dear. This, of course, has already taken place. Psychoanalysis in the form of that dissemination of itself that Freud called the therapy for the people everywhere exists. The child seeing the school counsellor, the patient with the clinical psychologist doing "self-esteem work," the analysand in psychoanalysis, even—all receive that positivized copper-gold alloy that Giegerich has called "psychology as the study of persons who '*have*' such and such a psychology"[70] in the form of a cornucopia of sociological, anthropological, and humanistic clichés. In professional journals, lifestyle magazines, and television talk shows (to say nothing of what comes out of our own mouths as we talk to one another), information regarding this issue or that syndrome are psycho-educationally dispensed.

Against this trend, true psychology, wherever practised, starts, as Giegerich said yesterday in the discussion period between lectures, ever and again *"from scratch."* Keeping to Jung's principle about not letting

---

[69] Sigmund Freud, "Lines of Advance in Psycho-Analytic Therapy," *The Standard Edition of the Complete Psychological Works of Sigmund Freud*, ed. & tr. J. Strachey (London: Hogarth Press, 1953-73), vol. 17, pp. 167-168.

[70] Giegerich, *The Soul's Logical Life*, pp. 22, 123, 172, 194, 195, 204, 212, 214, 251. The passage I have quoted here is my amalgamation of various expressions in the pages just listed.

anything from outside get in, it eschews what psychology thinks it already knows, in order to in each case get to the particular prime matter at hand and to exist as its unfolding. For only by falling into the eachness and inner infinity of the matter at hand (or as Findlay says, by ascending from the springboard of its negation), can the Mercurius within it be found.

As for copper and gold, suggestion and analysis, much the same can be said of these that I said in my previous lecture of mud and water. The point is not to keep them apart in their abstract purity or isolated difference. Still less is it to alloy them together in a compromise formation, as Freud recommends. For that, too, is a contradiction; indeed, a most intolerable one given that psychoanalysis began as much with the pushing off from suggestion (Freud's early work in hypnosis) as it did from a pushing off from the seduction theory. No, the challenge as always is tautegorically to *think* the contradictory unity of their identity and difference and, by precisely this dialectical means, to ascend to that most negative form of their *coniunctio*, speculative thought, true psychology. Pushing off from the positivity of its base in the methods of the empirical sciences, psychology, as Giegerich has said, must think on its own authority, out of the depth of its own notion of itself, both speculatively and rigorously at once.

* * * *

A final reflection. Freud's reference to copper and gold calls to mind another analytic forebear and another metal. I refer here to Hillman and his writings on silver. Valorizing in Bachelardian fashion the silver of the alchemists as the metal of imagining, Hillman, in "Silver and the White Earth," writes:

> What is reflection then when there is no subject reflected, neither emotion nor external object? No fact at all? The very idea of reflection transmutes from witness of a phenomenon, a mirroring of something else, to a resonance of the phenomena itself, a metaphor without a referent, or better said, an image.[71]

---

[71] James Hillman, "Silver and the White Earth (part one), *Spring 1980: An Annual of Archetypal Psychology and Jungian Thought* (Dallas: Spring Publications, 1980), pp. 45-46.

Returning to this theme a year later in part two of his essay, Hillman continues his silvery insight:

> Mental events as images do not require and cannot acquire further validation by virtue of exteriority. The soul's life is not upheld as correct by virtue of exteriority. But neither are mental events validated by virtue of my 'having' a dream, 'thinking' an idea or 'feeling' an experience.[72]

In these passages, Hillman well conveys the negativity of the image, its silvery interiorization into itself. But what of the gold that is to follow?[73] In Giegerich's view, the "gold" of true psychology is the further negation of the image's silvery negativity into the absolute negativity of a consciousness that can *think* the various moments of each image all at once. Like the alchemical "stone that is not a stone," the dialectical gold arising negatively out of silver and imagination is no longer *gold* any more (for that is only how silver had imaginatively pictured it in advance of its even subtler arrival); rather, it is logical form, absolute-negative interiority, spirit, thought.

---

[72] James Hillman, "Silver and the White Earth (part two), *Spring 1981: An Annual of Archetypal Psychology and Jungian Thought* (Dallas: Spring Publications, 1981), pp. 49-50.
[73] For Hillman's treatment of the culminating stage of the alchemical opus, see his "Concerning the Stone: Alchemical Images of the Goal," *Sphinx 5* (London: London Convivium for Archetypal Studies, 1993), pp. 234-65.

Afterword

Wolfgang Giegerich

This book contains the prepared lectures that were given at the El Capitan Canyon Seminar. What it does not present is the lively discussions that were an essential part of the seminar. This oral aspect cannot be reconstructed and represented in this book. But to somehow pay tribute to this part of the seminar, too, I want to give attention to one of the issues of dissension that came up, one that is crucial for my thesis and the topic of this whole book.

But before I come to that, I want to express my gratitude to my colleagues David Miller and Greg Mogenson for their willingness to join me in this adventure, for their sincere dedication to the subject matter that brought us together, for their immense support before and during the event, for their didactic skills, and for the good spirit that they brought to the event and with which they were present at it. David Miller's teaching in the months before not only prepared the ground for the possibility that such a seminar could be envisioned in the first place; his prior teaching was of course also to a large degree responsible for its actual success. The e-mail exchanges with Greg Mogenson before the event and also afterwards, in connection with the preparation of this book and his function as editor, were stimulating and rewarding. And then of course I want to thank *and compliment* the participants of the El Capitan Canyon seminar. It was their serious intellectual motivation that persuaded me to accept their invitation. The organization, mainly by Sharon Allen and Joshua Bertetta and their helpers, was perfect, no small feat and a very important precondition for our wholehearted concentration on intellectual themes. And the attitude, the lively interest, even enthusiasm, the engaged working spirit with which the participants actively entered into discussions made this seminar not only a most satisfying teaching experience, but also a truly remarkable event, as David Miller has already shown in his Introduction.

The one issue of dissension to be taken up here can be expressed in the following critical questions:

Would we not, with my emphasis on thought and on "logical life," betray the soul? Would we not leave the "vale of soul-making" and instead ascend into the heights of abstractions and to "the peaks of spirit"? Is the imagination not, and does it not have to be, the privileged access to what can rightly be called "soul" and "soulful"? Because, when Jung states "image is soul" (CW 13 § 75, transl. modified), does this not at the same time imply the converse statement that soul IS image? In other words, did Jung not tell us here that "image" is the innermost nature of soul? If so, when we try to go beyond "image" to thought, do we not necessarily turn our back on the soul?

It cannot be the purpose of the following remarks to try to refute such suspicions nor to persuade those who hold them. Quite apart from the fact that I do not want to turn this afterword into another paper attempting to discuss these questions exhaustively—such an intention would also be illusionary because psychological positions are not fully accessible to argumentation inasmuch as they express personal vested interests: the "psychology that one *has*," "that one *is*," "that one lives." All I can hope to do is to clarify for myself my own position concerning these important issues.

In his Introduction, David Miller pointed to the problems I see with the "effect of splitting *anima* from *animus* ..." and has already made it very clear that my pleading for "thought" is not a call to turn our backs on "image" and on what archetypal theorizing had accomplished, "but rather to continue it radically in an attempt to complete it ..." And in the following comments on the question of "thought versus soul" I want to continue this line of thought.

There are obviously two possible ways to think the relation between these two. The one way, operative in the set of critical questions cited above, construes the relation as an alternative, a choice: soul or spirit, image or thought, vale or peak, anima or animus. It is a thinking in terms of otherness and externality: the one has the other outside of itself. What I offer instead is a psychology of interiority. There are not two, but only one, and this "one" contains its own "other" within itself. Thought is not an external other to the image, but it is the very "soul" of the image itself; the image is, as it were, the external garment of the thought, just as a psychosomatic symptom or an acting-out behavior is the external surface of an image that remains more or less completely concealed within what explicitly manifests. The spirit in my sense is not what requires that you leave the vale of soul-making behind in order to climb into the thin air of mountain peaks; to express it in alchemical imagery, it is rather the mercurial spirit imprisoned in the imaginal matter (or the matter of the imagination); anima and animus do not coexist side by side like sister and brother, nor like two opponents, but the anima has the animus as its own "Bluebeard-killer" or "Hades-rapist" within itself.

The reference to "Bluebeard" and "killing" or "Hades" and "rape" is important, because the relation between soul (or image) and thought is decisively not a harmless one. Thought indeed robs the image of its virginal innocence. The one *is* the negation of the other. *However*: the point is that this violence is not done to the image (or soul) by an external other, but comes from within itself, and as its own telos.

Here everything depends on whether we *think* this "within itself" or merely imagine it pictorially. In the latter case we would not really have progressed beyond the external view, for even the "within itself" could still be imagined in terms of an external opposition; just think of dangerous bacteria or viruses that are deep within our bodies but are nevertheless just as much enemies as are threats from outside.

How does "thought" "kill" the innocence of the image from within the image itself and thus *as the image's own doing*? How can the animus be the "killer" of the anima and yet not be external to her, but her very own inner "self"? The answer lies in the notion of "self-application" that I made use of in the discussion of the glass-mountain tale above.

As I see it, the problem with imaginal psychology is that it stops halfway. It merely *views*, attends to, and appreciates, the image *before* itself. It thus carries the image before itself like a monstrance (in Roman Catholicism the precious vessel in which the priest holds up the consecrated Host for adoration), thereby preserving both it and itself in their virginal intactness and immediacy. Paradoxically, precisely by "adoring" the image, so to speak, in this way, imaginal psychology does not take it entirely seriously. The imagining mind reserves itself. In order to do full justice to the image, we have to go all the way, instead of tender-mindedly holding the image in front of us, always maintaining the difference and distance between consciousness and image as object or content of consciousness. We have to be *really* serious about the image and go through with it: apply what it is about (what its innermost message is) to itself. It has to take its own medicine, and it wants, longs, to take its own medicine, because only in this way can it find its fulfillment. Whereas a monstrance is like an unopened, unread, albeit *holy* book, the image that has been applied to itself or has come home to itself is like a book when it has been read.

The image needs *us* so that *it* can be thought. We must come up to it, penetrate "the monstrance" that it was at first. But in its being thought by us it merely thinks itself. And *we* need the *image*, need to think it, because only in our working with it and thinking it can the mind distill, sublimate, refine itself.

Semantically, the imagining mind has no problem entertaining horrible images like those of Hades raping Kore or of Bluebeard murdering his wives, images in which the one opposite indeed comes cruelly home to the other. But the imagining mind leaves the event of negation that is the content of those images out there, as the semantic content of the image. It freezes and locks the self-movement of the image in the image, on the semantic level. *Within* the image, he, Hades, does something to her, Kore. But there the imagining mind stops. It does not allow the content of the image (the negation of virginal innocence) to come home to the imaginal *form* of the image itself and, which is the same thing, to the logical *form* of consciousness, to the mind's innocently *imagining* the image, its "*dreaming* the myth onwards."

Therefore, when the imagining mind wants to think the relation of soul and thought *as such*, i.e., its (the mind's) own *syntax*, what was true inside the image is here no longer true. Instead of *experiencing* (suffering) the negating, putrefying work of its own inner other upon itself from within itself, this mind, in order to imagine the relation between soul and thought, resorts to a spatial imagination in terms of Cartesian *extensio*, for example to the essentially immobile images of peaks and vales, two separate places in an imaginal geography. In this way each is by definition, and so for eternity, kept away from the other, a conjunction or a working of the one upon the other being absolutely precluded. And in addition, the imagining mind positions itself in the vales, the one side only of its own whole alternative. Through this one-sidedness it reverses the relation: it expels ("extra-verts") that which is actually its own internal, but *active-subversive*, other, its own "soul," so that the latter now appears to be an external other vis-à-vis itself, out there, up there; at the same time, having freed itself of its internal other and thus of its own garment or surface character, it feels fully independent in its own right and already complete as it is; and it has now itself taken charge of the negating activity (the addressee of which it was meant to be) and acts it out upon the externalized other side of its own alternative (that normally would conversely have been its own inner fermenting-corrupting agent), simply by keeping it out and away as of no concern to it.

The other way around: only because it positioned itself one-sidedly in the vales does it also have to *imagine* the relation between soul and thought, to set it up as an external and static difference in spatial terms. The imagination is intrinsically "extraverted" (in a psychological, not personalistic, sense). And as long as the mind takes the imagination as its horizon, it has to choose: either vale or peak, either soul-making or lofty spiritual aspirations (where both, even the spiritual path, are equally children of the vale or anima position; it is, after all, the anima that conceives of spirit sentimentally and mindlessly as 'lofty spirituality.' This is how the anima *imagines* its other. And those who practice this kind of spirituality are doing so on the basis of an anima position, only that they try, *within* the anima mentality, to rise above the vale of the anima. But the anima standpoint does not have an inkling of what the anima's real other, what concrete spirit is, 'absolute' spirit, spirit absolved from the opposition of peak and vale: spirit as the mercurial soul of *all* reality).

Having to choose is the problem of the anima. You cannot be at two topoi in imaginal geography at once. The syzygial unity (the unity of unity and difference) of image and thought, anima and animus, cannot be *imagined*, nor can the soul's interiority; like Moses, the imagination necessarily remains outside the Promised Land. The fact that the imagination qua imagination *has to* imagine the relation as an *alternative* (e.g., of peak *versus* vale) merely reflects the inherent deficiency of the mode of imagining itself. Through its deficiency, the imagination points beyond itself.

In this way the imagining mind tries to assure its own innocence and to keep the image (regardless of how "violent" a coniunctio it may be about semantically, content-wise) in the status of a kind of "monstrance." Imaginal psychology, wittingly or not, insists on being "anima-only" psychology. But as anima-only psychology it is paradoxically a (certainly different) type of ego or personalistic psychology: the *empirical person* practices the soulful, "soul-making" imagination of the image as his or her doing (his or her acting out), so that the mind or soul itself, its logical constitution, gets away unscathed and does not have to *er-innern* (interiorize) the very message of the images it entertains, does not have to allow their content to come home to the imaginal form. Here, in the realm of its "syntax," the soul stays Kore forever, delighting in the flowers of the imaginal. It never turns into Persephone. To quote Hegel, "Impotent Beauty hates the Understanding for asking of her what she cannot do."

The soulful image deserves better and more.

A Bibliography of the Works of Wolfgang Giegerich

I. Books

1987f* *Der Verlorene Sohn. Vom Ursprung des Dichtens Wilhelm Raabes* (Wilhelm Raabe-Studien Bd. 3, ed. Otto Huth), Essen (Die Blaue Eule) 1987.

1988b *Die Atombombe als seelische Wirklichkeit. Ein Versuch über den Geist des christlichen Abendlandes.* Erster Band der "Psychoanalyse der "tombombe". Mit einem Geleitwort von Herbert Pietschmann, Zürich (Schweizer Spiegel Verlag, Raben-Reihe) 1988.

1989a *Drachenkampf oder Initiation ins Nuklearzeitalter.* Zweiter Band der "Psychoanalyse der Atombombe", Zürich (Schweizer Spiegel Verlag, Raben-Reihe) 1989.

1993e *Tötungen. Gewalt aus der Seele: Versuch über Ursprung und Geschichte des Bewußtseins*, Frankfurt/M, Berlin, Bern, New York, Paris, Wien (Peter Lang) 1994.

1993f *Animus-Psychologie*, Frankfurt/M, Berlin, Bern, New York, Paris, Wien (Peter Lang) 1994.

1998a *The Soul's Logical Life: Towards a Rigorous Notion of Psychology*, Frankfurt am Main, Berlin, Bern, New York, Paris, Wien (Peter Lang) 1998, 5th rev. ed. 2019.

1999a *Der Jungsche Begriff der Neurose*, Frankfurt/M, Berlin, Bern, New York, Paris, Wien (Peter Lang), 1999.

2000b *Tamashî to Rekishisei* (Yungu Shinrigaku no Tenkai [Gîgerihhi

---

* Letters after years indicate the order in which works were published within the year in question.

	Ronshû], 1) [= *The Soul and Historicity* (Die Entfaltung der Jungschen Psychologie [Papers by Giegerich], Vol. 1)], transl. and ed. Toshio Kawai, Tokyo (Nihon Hyôron-sha) 2000.
2001b	*Shinwa to Ishiki* (Yungu Shinrigaku no Tenkai [Gîgerihhi Ronshû], 3) [= *Mythos und Bewußtsein* (Die Entfaltung der Jungschen Psychologie [Papers by Giegerich], Vol. 3)], transl. and ed. Toshio Kawai, Tokyo (Nihon Hyôron-sha) 2001.
2004f	*Il Concetto di Nevrosi secondo Jung. Dall' esperienza personale alla riflessione*, (= *Der Jungsche Begriff der Neurose*, Itaian.), transl. Maria Irmgard Wuehl, Milano (La biblioteca di Vivarium) 2004.
2005d	(with David L. Miller, Greg Mogenson) *Dialectics and Analytical Psychology: The El Capitan Canyon Seminar*, New Orleans (Spring Journal Books) 2005.
2005g	*La Fine del Senso e la Nascita dell' Uomo. Sullo Stato raggiunto nella Storia della Coscienza. Un' Analisi del Progetto psicologico di C. G. Jung*, Milano (la biblioteca di Vivarium) 2005, transl. Maria Irmgard Wuehl.
2006c	*The Neurosis of Psychology. Primary Papers towards a Critical Psychology.* (= W. G., Collected English Papers, vol. 1) New Orleans (Spring Journal Books) 2006.
2007d	*Technology and the Soul. From the Nuclear Bomb to the World Wide Web.* (= W. G., Collected English Papers, vol. 2) New Orleans (Spring Journal Books) 2007.
2008d	*Alchimia della Storia e la morte dell' anima nella civiltà della tecnica.* With an Introduction by Eva Pattis, Bergamo (Moretti & Vitali) 2008.
2008h	*Soul-Violence.* (= W. G., Collected English Papers, vol. 3) New Orleans (Spring Journal Books) 2008.
2010d	*La vita logica dell'anima. Verso una nozione rigorosa di psicologia*, transl. Luciano Paoli, Milano (La Biblioteca di Vivarium) 2010.
2010j	*The Soul Always Thinks.* (= W. G., Collected English Papers, vol. 4) New Orleans (Spring Journal Books) 2010.
2012e	*What Is Soul?* New Orleans (Spring Journal Books) 2012.
2013a	*Gīgerihhi yume seminā* (= *Giegerich Dream Seminar*, Japanese), ed. by Toshio Kawai and Yasuhiro Tanaka, with a preface and notes by Toshio Kawai, Osaka (Sogen-sha Publisher) 2013.
2013d	*The Flight into the Unconscious. An Analysis of C. G. Jung's*

Psychology Project (= W. G., Collected English Papers, vol. 5) New Orleans, LA (Spring Journal Books) 2013.

2013i   *Neurosis. The Logic of a Metaphysical Illness*, New Orleans, LA (Spring Journal Books) 2013.

2014a   *"Dreaming the Myth Onwards": C. G. Jung on Christianity and on Hegel. Part 2 of The Flight Into the Unconscious* (= W. G., Collected English Papers, vol. 6) New Orleans, LA (Spring Journal Books) 2013.

2018b   *Pitfalls in Comparing Buddhist and Western Psychology: A contribution to psychology's self-clarification*, ISPDI Monograph Series, vol. 2, CreateSpace Independent Publishing Platform, 2018.

2018c   *Tamashii no Ronriteki Seimei—Shinrigaku no Genmitsuna Gainen ni Mukete* (= *The Soul's Logical Life*, Japanese), transl. Yasuhiro Tanaka, Osaka, Sogensha Publishers, 2018.

II. Papers and Occasional Writings

A. German

1969   "'Der verlorene Sohn'. Vom Ursprung des Dichtens Wilhelm Raabes", in: *Dissertation abstracts 29*, 1968/69, 4455A.

1971   "Dumas' 'Le Comte de Monte-Christo' und Wilhelm Raabe", in: *Jahrbuch der Raabe-Gesellschaft 1971*, Braunschweig, pp. 49-71.

1977b   "Die wissenschaftliche Psychologie als subjektivistische und zudeckende Psychologie", in: *Analyt. Psychol. 8* (1977), pp. 262-283.

1978a   "Die Gegenwart als Dimension der Seele - Aktualkonflikt und archetypische Psychotherapie", in: *Analyt. Psychol. 9* (1978), pp. 99-110.

1978b   "Über die Neurose der Psychologie oder das Dritte der Zwei", in: *Analyt. Psychol. 9* (1978), pp. 241-268.

1979a   "Principium Individuationis und Individuationsprozeß", in: U. Eschenbach (ed.), *Die Behandlung in der Analytischen Psychologie I*, Fellbach (Bonz-Verlag) 1979, pp. 141-170.

1979b   "Der Sprung nach dem Wurf. Über das Einholen der Projektion

	und den Ursprung der Psychologie", in: *GORGO 1/1979*, pp. 49-71.
1979d	"Der Terrorismus als Aufgabe und Verantwortung. Überlegungen eines Tiefenpsychologen", in: *Analyt. Psychol. 10* (1979), pp. 190-215.
1980a	"Streit", in: *Analyt. Psychol. 11* (1980), pp. 18-37.
1980b	"Beitrag zur Polytheismus-Diskussion", in: *GORGO 2/1979*, pp. 62-69.
1981a	Review of: Hans-Dieter Schwind (ed.), *Ursachen des Terrorismus in der Bundesrepublik Deutschland*, in: *Analyt. Psychol. 12* (1981), pp. 157-158.
1981b	"Die Rettung des Kindes oder die Entwendung der Zeit", in: *GORGO 5/1981*, pp. 9-32.
1983a	"Wildnis und Geborgenheit. Das Konsultationszimmer als Ort der Psychotherapie", in: *Analyt. Psychol. 14* (1983), Sie. 108-125.
1983b	"Buße für Philemon: Vertiefung in das verdorbene Gast-Spiel der Götter", in: *Eranos 51-1982*, Frankfurt (Insel) 1983, pp. 189-242.
1983c	"Die Bedeutung des Körpers in Psychologie und Psychotherapie", in: *Analyt. Psychol. 14* (1983), pp. 264-284.
1984a	"Gotteserfahrung—psychologisch gesehen", in: *Herrenalber Texte 51* (ed. by W. Böhme), 1984, pp. 83-102.
1984b	"Die Herkunft der wissenschaftlichen Erkenntnisse C. G. Jungs", in: *GORGO 7/JG. 4* (1984), pp. 1-31.
1984c	"Die Selbstgenügsamkeit des Jeweiligen. Zu Ulrich Manns Antwort auf James Hillmans Buch über Pan", in: *Analyt. Psychol. 15* (1984), pp. 182-200.
1985a	"Lichtsymbolik 1984", in: *Institutsbrief Nr. 2*, Febr. 1985, C. G. Jung-Institut-Stuttgart, pp. 24-25.
1985b	"Das Begräbnis der Seele in die technische Zivilisation", in: *Eranos 52-1983*, pp. 211-276.
1985c	"Atombombe und Seele", in: *Integrative Therapie 4/1984*, pp. 341-367.
1985d	"Das Goldene Kalb, der goldene Blitz", in: *Deutsches Allgemeines Sonntagsblatt Nr. 23*, 9. Juni 1985, "Magazin" pp. XI.
1985e	"Der Tanz um das Goldene Kalb. Gedanken über Gott und

Götzen im Schatten der Atombombe", in: Peter-Michael Pflüger (ed.), *Apokalyptische Ängste und psychosoziale Wirklichkeit*, Fellbach (Bonz-Verlag) 1985, pp. 123-168.

1985i   "Editorial", in: *GORGO 9/1985*, pp. 1-3.

1985j   "Die Erlösung aus dem Strom des Geschehens. Okeanos und der Blutkreislauf", in: *GORGO 9/1985*, pp. 35-55.

1986a   "Atombombe und Seele", in: H. Petzold (ed.), *Psychotherapie und Friedensarbeit*, Reihe Innovative Psychotherapie und Humanwissenschaften Bd. 32, Paderborn (Junfermann) 1986, pp. 127-159.

1987c   "Die Alchemie der Geschichte", in: *Eranos 54-1985*, Frankfurt (Insel) 1987, pp. 325-395.

1987d   "Die Bodenlosigkeit der Jungschen Psychologie. Über unsere Identität als Jungianer", in: *GORGO 12/1987*, pp. 43-62.

1987e   "Die Bodenlosigkeit der Jungschen Psychologie. Zur Frage unserer Identität als Jungianer" (Autoreferat), in: *Jahresbericht 1986/87* Psychologischer Club Zürich, pp. 24-25.

1987g   "Die Exercitia spiritualia des Ignatius von Loyola und die Unterschiede zwischen einer 'theologischen' und einer 'psychologischen' Einstellung zur religiösen Erfahrung", in: *Analyt. Psychol. 18* (1987), pp. 105-134.

1987l   "Editorial", in: *GORGO 13/1987*, p. 3.

1988c   "Das Bewußtsein, der zweite Schöpfer der Welt", in: *Eranos 55-1986*, Frankfurt (Insel) 1988, pp. 183-239.

1988d   "Editorial", in: *GORGO 14/1988*, pp. 3-4.

1988e   "Zur Form der Differenz von Psychologie und Theologie. Antwort auf Ulrich Manns kritische Gegenfragen", in: *Analyt. Psychol. 19 (1988)*, pp. 223-228.

1988i   (Editorial), in: *GORGO 15/1988*, p. 4.

1988j   "Zuerst Schatten, dann Anima. Oder: Die Ankunft des Gastes. Schattenintegration und die Entstehung der Psychologie", in: *GORGO 15/1988*, pp. 5-28.

1988k   "Bibliographie Heino Gehrts", in: *GORGO 15/1988*, pp. 59-62.

1989b   "Der Doppelschritt: Vom Buchstäblichen über das Imaginale zum Konkret-Wirklichen. Eine Antwort an Frau Vetter-Lüscher", in: *GORGO 16/1989*, pp. 60-67.

1989d   Review of: Toshio Kawai, *Bild und Sprache und ihre Beziehung zur Welt. Überlegungen zur Bedeutung von Jung und Heidegger für die Psychologie*, in: *Analyt. Psychol.* 20 (1989), pp. 321-323.

1989e   "Metakritik an den Kommentaren in *GORGO* 16 zu Hillmans 'Vom Spiegel zum Fenster'", in: *GORGO 17/1989*, pp. 51-61.

1990a   "Die Abwehr des Schattens", in: Guggenbühl, A.; Kunz, M. (Eds.), *Das Schreckliche: Mythologische Betrachtungen zum Abgründigen im Menschen*, Zürich (Schweizer Spiegel Verlag, Raben-Reihe) 1990, pp. 17-32.

1990c   "Die Syzygie. Über die Wirklichkeit der Welt oder die Not der Psychologie", in: *Eranos 57-1988*, Frankfurt (Insel) 1990, pp. 235-305.

1991c   "'Aphrodites Wiedergeburt' oder der Betrug: Zur psychologischen Rede von Göttern", appeared in print with the unauthorized altered title: "Vom Reden über Götter: ein psychologischer Betrug" in: *GORGO 20/1991*, pp. 7-28.

1991e   "Apokalypse des verschlossenen Lichts", in: Peter Sloterdijk u. Thomas H. Macho (ed.), *Weltreligion der Seele. Ein Lese- und Arbeitsbuch der Gnosis von der Spätantike bis zur Gegenwart*, 2. Bd., ohne Ort (Artemis & Winkler) 1991, pp. 601-604. [Auszug aus: d41 (=58) 1989a].

1992c   "Tötungen: Über Gewalt aus der Seele", in: *Gewalt - warum? Der Mensch: Zerstörer und Gestalter*, ed. Peter M. Pflüger, Olten and Freiburg (Walter) 1992, pp. 184-233 and 240-243.

1993a   "Die Alchemie der Geschichte - I. Die Erlösung von der Geschichte: Historismus, Naturwissenschaft, Psychologie", *GORGO 24/1993*, pp. 39-66.

1993d   "Die Alchemie der Geschichte. II. Die Einbindung in die Geschichte: Kafkas 'Strafkolonie'", *GORGO 25/1993*, pp. 17-47.

1994b   "Effizienz- statt Existenzbeweis der Psychologie: Ein jungianischer Schildbürgerstreich", *GORGO 26/1994*, pp. 37-60.

1994d   "Die Alchemie der Geschichte. II. Die Einbindung in die Geschichte: Kafkas 'Strafkolonie' / L'alchimia della storia. II. L'incorporamento nella storia: La 'Colonia penale' di Kafka", transl. Anna Accogli, in: *l'immaginale 17* (October 1994) pp. 124-183.

1995b	"Blockflötenklänge. Zu Rudolf Müllers 'Si tacuisses...: Wie Wolfgang Giegerich versucht den Mond zu fangen'", in: *Analytische Psychologie 26* 1995, pp. 133-138.
1996b	"Die Rettung des Kindes oder die Entwendung der Zeit / La salvezza del bambino o la sottrazione del tempo", transl. Anna Accogli, in: *l'imaginale 20* (April 1996), pp. 96-143.
1996c	"Die Entstehung des Menschen aus dem Opfer", in: *Orientierung: Berichte und Analysen aus der Arbeit der Evangelischen Akademie Nordelbien* 2/1996, pp. 38-51.
1997b	"Die Herkunft der psychologischen Erkenntnisse C. G. Jungs / L'origine delle conoscenze psicologiche di C. G. Jung", transl. Anna Accogli, in: *l'imaginale 22* (April 1997), pp. 38-95.
1997e	"Der Mythos vom Mythos im Alltag", in: *GORGO 33/1997*, pp. 5-26.
1998c	"Der Mythos vom Mythos im Alltag / Il mito dal mito alla vita quotidiana", transl. Anna Accogli, in: *l'imaginale 24* (April 1998), pp. 4-41.
1999c	"Principium Individuationis und Individuationsprozeß / Principium individuationis e processo di individuazione", transl. Pasquale Mauro, in: *l'imaginale 26* (April 1999), pp. 66-115.
2000c	"Umweltträume? Zu N.F. Patzel: Träume angehender Umweltwissenschaftler", in: *GAIA 9/1 (2000)*, pp. 5.
2000h	"Das World Wide Web aus der Sicht des logischen Lebens der Seele", transl. Axel Holm, in: *GORGO 39/2000*, pp. 5-28.
2002d	"Der Gegensatz von 'individuell' und 'kollektiv'—die Grundstörung der Psychologie: Reflexionen über das 'magnum opus' der Seele heute", transl. Axel Holm, in: *GORGO 43/2002*, pp. 35-62.
2004c	"[Ein kleines Licht, durch Nacht und Sturm zu tragen.] Zur Lage der Jungschen Psychologie heute. / A Little Light to Be Carried Through Night and Storm. Comments on the State of Jungian Psychology Today", in: Dieter Klein and Henning Weyerstraß (eds.), *Auf den Spuren von C. G. Jung - In Search of C. G. Jung*, Köln (Verlag dieterklein.com) 2004, pp. 33-36.
2005b	"Was heilt?", in: *Heilkräfte. 7. Symposium der Paracelsus Akademie Villach*, Villach (KI-Esoterik Verlag) 2005, pp. 33-62.

2005c (Untitled) Beitrag zu einer Podiumsdiskussion, zusammen mit Hans-Ulrich Grimm, Rotraud A. Perner, Werner Freudenberger, in: *Heilkräfte. 7. Symposium der Paracelsus Akademie Villach*, Villach (KI-Esoterik Verlag) 2005, pp. 63-95.

2005f (With others) Antworten auf eine Umfrage: "Hat die Tiefenpsychologie eine Zukunft? Thesen und Fragen zur aktuellen Zukunft der archetypischen/Jungschen Psychologie", in: *GORGO 48/2005*, pp. 5-24.

2006f "Das verdrängte Vergessen. Auschwitz und die sogenannte 'Erinnerungskultur'", in: GORGO 50 / 2006, pp. 21-42.

2010k "Der rituelle Maskentanz und die Lehre, die er enthält", in: Ursula Steinbach (ed.), *Danke, Bert. Festschrift zum 85. Geburtstag von Bert Hellinger*, ism-Institut für Systemaufstellung und Meditation, Kassel 2010, pp.156-164.

2014c "Neurose: das Werk der kranken Seele", in: *Analytische Psychologie* Heft 177, 45. Jg. 3/2014, pp. 288-300.

2016b "Vorwort", in: Heino Gehrts, *Initiation, Einweihungsrituale und Wesensphänomene*, ed. by Heiko Fritz, Schriften zur Märchen-, Mythen- und Sagenforschung Band 3, Gesammelte Aufsätze 3, Hamburg (Igel Verlag) 1916, pp. 5-22.

2018d "Geist und Seele. C. G. Jung und die psychologische Differenz", in: *Analytische Psychologie* Heft 190, 2/2018, 49. Jg., pp. 214-254.

B. English

1975 "Ontogeny = Phylogeny? A Fundamental Critique of E. Neumann's Analytical Psychology", in: *Spring 1975*, pp. 110-129.

1977a "On the Neurosis of Psychology or The Third of the Two", in: *Spring 1977*, pp. 153-174.

1979c "Postscript to Cocks", in: *Spring 1979*, pp. 228-231.

1984d "Hospitality Toward the Gods in an Ungodly Age. Philemon—Faust—Jung", in: *Spring 1984*, pp. 61-75.

1985g "The Nuclear Bomb and the Fate of God", in: *Spring 1985*, pp. 1-27.

1985h "Comment on 'The Autonomous Psyche. A Communication to Goodheart from the Bi-Personal Field of Paul Kugler and James Hillman'", in: *Spring 1985*, pp. 172-174.

1986b	"The Rescued Child or the Misappropriation of Time—On the Search for Meaning" (= "Die Rettung des Kindes oder die Entwendung der Zeit", English), transl. from the original German by Gertrud Mander, in: *Harvest 32* (1986), pp. 7-25.
1987a	"Saving the Nuclear Bomb", in: V. Andrews, R. Bosnak, and K. W. Goodwin (eds.), *Facing Apocalypse*, Dallas (Spring Publications) 1987, pp. 96-108.
1987h	"The Rescue of the World. Jung, Hegel, and the Subjective Universe", in: *Spring 1987*, pp. 107-114.
1987j	"The Nuclear Bomb as a Psychological Reality", in: K. Porter, D. Rinzler, and P. Olsen (eds.), *Heal or Die. Psychotherapists Confront Nuclear Annihilation*, New York (Psychohistory Press) 1987, pp. 84-98.
1987k	"Jungian Psychology: A Baseless Enterprise. Reflections on Our Identity as Jungians", in: *Harvest 33* (1987-88), pp. 91-103.
1987	Roberts Avens, "Reflections on Wolfgang Giegerich's 'The Burial of the Soul in Technological Civilization'", in: *Sulfur 20* (Fall 1987), pp. 34-54. [Detailed English summary of German 1985b].
1988a	"Deliverance from the Stream of Events: Okeanos and the Circulation of the Blood", in: *Sulfur 21* (Winter 1988), pp. 118-140.
1988f	"The Invention of Explosive Power and the Blueprint of the Bomb—A Chapter in the Imaginal Pre-history of Our Nuclear Predicament", in: *Spring 1988*, pp. 1-14.
1988g	"Effort? Yes, Effort!", in: *Spring 1988*, pp. 181-188.
1988h	"Rupture. Or: Psychology and Religion", in: *Zen Buddhism Today*. Annual Report of the Kyoto Zen Symposium, No. 6, November 1988, Kyoto, Japan (The Kyoto Seminar for Religious Philosophy), pp. 39-49.
1991a	"The Rocket and the Launching Base. Or: The Leap from the Imaginal Into the Outer Space Named 'Reality'", in: *Sulfur 28* (Spring 1991), pp. 62-78.
1991d	"The Advent of the Guest: Shadow Integration and the Rise of Psychology", in: *Spring 51* (1991), pp. 86-106.
1992a	"The Fabrication of Time", in: *Sulfur 30* (Spring 1992), pp. 46-58.

1992e "Ontogeny = Phylogeny? A Fundamental Critique of E. Neumann's Analytical Psychology", in: Renos K. Papadopoulos (ed.), *Carl Gustav Jung: Critical Assessments*, Vol. II, London (Routledge) 1992, pp. 138-155.

1992f "Jungian Psychology: A Baseless Enterprise. Reflections on Our Identity as Jungians", in: Renos K. Papadopoulos (ed.), *Carl Gustav Jung: Critical Assessments*, Vol. IV, London (Routledge) 1992, pp. 393-406.

1993c "Killings: Psychology's Platonism and the Missing Link to Reality", in: *Spring 54* (June 1993), pp. 5-18.

1994a "Asher's Communitarian Self", in: *Spring 55* (Spring 1994), pp. 145-155.

1995c "Letter to the Editor on Hillman's Reply to the Article 'Killings'", in: *Spring 57* (Spring, 1995), pp. 139-140.

1995d "Ending Emancipation from History: Kafka's 'In the Penal Colony'", transl. Susan Giegerich, in: *Sulfur 37* (Fall 1995), pp. 147-173.

1996d "The Opposition of 'Individual' and 'Collective'—Psychology's Basic Fault. Reflections on Today's *Magnum Opus* of the Soul / L'oppositione tra 'individuale' e 'collettivo'—l'errore di base della psicologia. Riflessioni sul *Magnum Opus* dell'Anima di oggi", transl. Anna Accogli, in: *l'imaginale 21* (October 1996), pp. 11-51.

1996e "The Opposition of 'Individual' and 'Collective'—Psychology's Basic Fault. Reflections on Today's *Magnum Opus* of the Soul", in: *Harvest*, vol. 42, no. 2 (1996), pp. 7-27.

1997a "The Dignity of Thought: In Defense of the Phenomenon of Philosophical Thought", in: *Harvest*, vol. 43, no.1 (1997), pp. 45-54.

1997c "The Opposition of 'Individual' and 'Collective' - Psychology's Basic Fault. Reflections On Today's *Magnum Opus* of the Soul", *Guild of Pastoral Psychology Lecture Pamphlet No. 259*, 1997.

1997f "Killings. The Relationship Between Sacrifices and Psyche", in: *The Salt Journal* (November / December 1997), pp. 39-43.

1998c "Jung's Betrayal of his Truth: The Adoption of a Kant-based Empiricism and the Rejection of Hegel's Speculative Thought", in: *Harvest*, vol. 44, no.1 (1998), pp. 46-64.

1999d	"The 'Patriarchal Neglect of the Feminine Principle': A Psychological Fallacy in Jungian Theory", in: *Harvest,* vol. 45, no. 1 (1999), pp. 7-30.
1999e	"Is the Soul 'Deep?'—Entering and Following the Logical Movement of Heraclitus' 'Fragment 45'", in: *Spring 64* (Fall and Winter 1998), pp. 1-32.
2000d	"The Lesson of the Mask", *Sulfur 45/46* (Spring 2000), pp. 109-113.
2000e	"Once More the Reality/Irreality Issue: A Reply to Hillman's Reply", in: http://www.rubedo.psc.br/reply.html.
2000g	"Is the Soul 'Deep?'—Entering and Following the Logical Movement of Heraclitus' 'Fragment 45'", in: *l'imaginale 28* (April 2000), pp. 4-63.
2001a	"The World Wide Web from the Point of View of the Soul's Logical Life / Il World Wide Web dal punto di vista della vita logica dell' anima", transl. Maria Teresa Trinchera, in: *l'imaginale 30* (April 2001), pp. 4-43.
2001c	"The Lesson of the Mask / La Lezione della Maschera", transl. Guiseppe Falco, in: *l'imaginale 31* (October 2001), pp. 4-13.
2002a	"Comments on Kenji Uzuki's 'An Approach to Understanding the Elements of Dreams'", in: *Sophia University Clinical Psychology Reports,* vol. 23 (2000), pp. 11-14.
2002c	"Islamic Terrorism", in: Luigi Zoja and Donald Williams (ed.), *Jungian Reflections on September 11: A Global Nightmare,* Einsiedeln (Daimon) 2002, pp. 57-80.
2003b	"The End of Meaning and the Birth of Man. An Essay about the State Reached in the History of Consciousness and an Analysis of C. G. Jung's Psychology Project", in: http://www.cgjungpage.org/articles/EndofMeaning.pdf.
2004a	"The End of Meaning and the Birth of Man: An Essay about the State Reached in the History of Consciousness and an Analysis of C. G. Jung's Psychology Project", in: *The Journal of Jungian Theory and Practice,* Vol. 6, No. 1, 2004, pp. 1-65.
2004b	"Response to the Responses by Mogenson, Miller, Beebe, and Pulver", in: *The Journal of Jungian Theory and Practice,* vol. 6, no. 1 (2004), pp. 107-124.

2004c "A Little Light to Be Carried Through Night and Storm. Comments on the State of Jungian Psychology Today", in: Dieter Klein and Henning Weyerstraß (eds.), *Auf den Spuren von C. G. Jung—In Search of C. G. Jung*, Köln (Verlag dieterklein.com) 2004, pp. 35-36.

2004d "The End of Meaning and the Birth of Man" [Lecture], *Guild of Pastoral Psychology, Guild Lecture No. 284*, [London] 2004.

2004d "After Shamdasani: *On Jung and the Making of Modern Psychology: The Dream of a Science* by Sonu Shamdasani", in: *Spring 71 (Orpheus): A Journal of Archetype and Culture* (Fall 2004), pp. 193-213.

2005e "Response to Sanford Drob", in: *Journal of Jungian Theory and Practice*, vol. 7, no. 1 (2005), pp. 55-58.

2006a "Once more 'The Stone Which is Not a Stone': Further Reflections on 'Not'", in: Christine Downing (ed.), *Disturbances in the Field: Essays in Honor of David L. Miller*, New Orleans (Spring Journal Books) 2006, pp. 127-141.

2006b "The Ego-Psychological Fallacy: A Note on 'the Birth of the Meaning out of a Symbol'", in: *Journal of Jungian Theory and Practice*, vol. 7, no. 2 (2005), pp. 53-59.

2006d "Closure and Setting Free, or The Bottled Spirit of Alchemy and Psychology", in: *Spring 74 (Alchemy): A Journal of Archetype and Culture* (Spring, 2006), pp. 31-62.

2006g "The Empirical Person Is Not the Subject of the Individuation Process. Interview with Wolfgang Giegerich", http://www.rubedo.psc.br/Entrevis/indgieg2.htm.

2006h "The Burial of the Soul in Technological Civilization", in: *Spring 75 (Psyche & Nature, Part 1 of 2): A Journal of Archetype and Culture* (Fall 2006), pp. 197-255.

2007c "Psychology—The Study of the Soul's Logical Life", in: Ann Casement (ed.), *Who Owns Jung?*, London (Karnac) 2007, pp. 247-263.

2007e "Psychology as Anti-Philosophy: C. G. Jung", in: *Spring 77 (Philosophy and Psychology): A Journal of Archetype and Culture* (June 2007), pp. 11-51.

2008e "'The Unassimilable Remnant'—What Is at Stake? A Dispute with Stanton Marlan", in: *Archetypal Psychologies: Reflections in*

Honor of James Hillman, New Orleans (Spring Journal Books) 2008, pp. 193-223.

2009f   "The Psychologist as Repentance Preacher and Revivalist: Robert Romanyshyn on the Melting of the Polar Ice", in: *Spring 82 (Symbolic Life 2009): A Journal of Archetype and Culture* (Fall 2009), pp. 193-221.

2010b   "Love the Questions Themselves", in: Robert and Janis Henderson, *Living with Jung: 'Enterviews' with Jungian Analysts*, Vol. 3, New Orleans (Spring Journal Books) 2010, pp. 263-302.

2010h   "*Liber Novus*, that is, The New Bible: A First Analysis of C. G. Jung's Red Book", in: *Spring 83 (Minding the Animal Psyche): A Journal of Archetype and Culture* (Spring 2010), pp. 361-411.

2011a   "God Must Not Die! C. G. Jung's Thesis of the One-Sidedness of Christianity", in: *Spring 84 (God Must Not Die! Or Must He?): A Journal of Archetype and Culture* (Fall 2010), pp. 11-71.

2012a   "The Disenchantment Complex: C. G. Jung and the Modern World", in: *International Journal of Jungian Studies,* vol. 4, no. 1 (March 2012), pp. 4-20.

2012g   "A Serious Misunderstanding: Synchronicity and the Generation of Meaning", in: *Journal of Analytical Psychology,* 57, (2012), pp. 500-511.

2012h   "Saban's Alternative. An Alternative?" in: http://ispdi.org/articles.html.

2014d   "Jungian Psychology as Metaphysics? A Response to Sean McGrath", in: *International Journal of Jungian Studies*, published online 15 September 2014; published in print in vol. 7, no. 3 (October 2015), pp. 242-250. DOI: 10.1080/19409052.2014.954438.

2015b   "Two Jungs. Apropos a Paper by Mark Saban", in: *Journal of Analytical Psychology*, vol. 60, no. 3 (2015), pp. 303-315.

2017a   "The 'Black Sun' Seen Through. Or: Marlan's Proton Pseudos", in: *ISPDI Newsletter,* March 2017.

2017b   "'Geist'. Or: What Gives Jungian Psychology Its Absolute Uniqueness and Is the Source of Its True Life", in: Jennifer M. Sandoval and John C. Knapp, (eds.), *Psychology as the Discipline of Interiority: 'The Psychological Difference' in the work of Wolfgang Giegerich*, London (Routledge) 2017, pp. 17-42.

2017d "The 'Black Sun' Seen Through. Or: Marlan's Proton Pseudos", revised and enlarged, in: http://www.ispdi.org/images/stories/PDFdocuments/Marlans_proton_pseudos_revised_1___1.pdf.

C. Italian

1985f "La nevrosi della psicologia o il terzo dei due", in: *l'immaginale. rassegna di psicologia immaginale 5* (1985), pp. 123-143.

1987b "Il presente come dimensione dell' anima. Conflitto attuale e psicoterapia archetipica", transl. Reinharda Grade, in: *l'immaginale 8* (1987), pp. 111-120.

1989c "La psicologia analitica e il pericolo nucleare", in: Paolo Aite and Aldo Carotenuto (eds.), *Itinerari del pensiero junghiano*, Mailand (Raffaello Cortina Editore) 1989, pp. 159-172.

1990b "L'ospitalità algi Dei in un mondo empio", transl. Paola Donfrancesco, in: *anima 3* (Spring 1990), pp. 5-24.

1991b "Liberazione dal fluire degli eventi: Okeanos e la circolazione sanguigna", in: Maria Teresa Colonna (ed.), *Percorsi del sogno. Rivista di Psicologia Analitica 43* (1991), pp. 187-213.

1992b "La costructione del tempo", transl. Marina Taccone, in: *l'immaginale 12* (April 1992), pp. 57-70.

1992d "Ontogenesi ' Filogenesi? Una Critica Fondamentale della Psicologia Analitica di Erich Neumann", transl. Marina Taccone, in: *l'immaginale 13* (October 1992), pp. 39-56.

1993b "Il salto dietro al lancio: sul recupero della proiezione e l'origine della psicologia", transl. Anna Accogli, in: *l'immaginale 14* (April 1993), pp. 83-103.

1994c "L'alchimia della storia. I. Liberazione della storia: Storicismo, scienze naturali, psicologia", transl. Anna Accogli, in: *l'immaginale 16* (April 1994), pp. 37-60.

1994d "L'alchimia della storia. II. L'incorporamento nella storia: La 'Colonia penale' di Kafka", transl. Anna Accogli, in: *l'immaginale 17* (Ottober 1994) pp. 124-183.

1995a "La psicologia junghiana, un'impresa senza fondamenta", transl. Bianca Garufi, in: *anima* (series 2, no. 3, 1995), pp. 144-158.

1995e "L'insediarsi dell'Anima Occidentale nella Caverna di Platone", in: *La Pratica Analytica 10/11* (1995), pp. 25-34.

1996a	"Integrazione dell'ombra e nascita della psicologia", transl. Paola Donfrancesco, in: *anima* (series 2, no. 4, 1996), pp. 137-155.
1996b	"La salvezza del bambino o la sottrazione del tempo", transl. Anna Accogli, in: *l'imaginale 20* (April 1996), pp. 96-143.
1996d	"L'oppositione tra 'individuale' e 'collettivo'—l'errore di base della psicologia. Riflessioni sul *Magnum Opus* dell'Anima di oggi", transl. Anna Accogli, in: *l'imaginale 21* (Ottober 1996), pp. 11-51.
1997b	"L'origine delle conoscenze psicologiche di C. G. Jung", transl. Anna Accogli, in: *l'imaginale 22* (April 1997), pp. 38-95.
1997d	"Riflessioni sulla frase di Jung '... d'ora in poi fino a un indeterminato futuro il vero problema sarà di ordine psicologico'", in: *contro tempo 2* (May 1997), pp. 93-110.
1998b	"*L'idea* junghiana del Sé nell'orizzonte della sua esperienza fondante", transl. Marta Ricci, in: *anima* 12 (1998), pp. 105-130 [The title is a mistranslation of "Jung's *thought* of the Self ...".]
1998c	"Il mito dal mito alla vita quotidiana", transl. Anna Accogli, in: *l'imaginale 24* (April 1998), pp. 4-41.
1999c	"Principium individuationis e processo di individuazione", transl. Pasquale Mauro, in: *l'imaginale 26* (April 1999), pp. 66-115.
2000g	"L'anima è 'profonda'?—Entrando e Seguendo il Movimento Logico del Frammento 45 di Eraclito", transl. Pasquale Mauro, in: *l'imaginale 28* (April 2000), pp. 4-63.
2001a	"The World Wide Web from the Point of View of the Soul's Logical Life / Il World Wide Web dal punto di vista della vita logica dell' anima", transl. Maria Teresa Trinchera, in: *l'imaginale 30* (April 2001), pp. 4-43.
2001c	"The Lesson of the Mask / La Lezione della Maschera", transl. Guiseppe Falco, in: *l'imaginale 31* (October 2001), pp. 4-13.
2002e	"Il terrorismo islamico" (= "Islamic Terrorism", Italian), transl. Luciano Perez, in: Luigi Zoja (ed.), *L'incubo globale*, Bergamo (Moretti & Vitali) 2002, pp. 85-104.
2003c	"L'ospitalità algi Dei in un mondo empio", transl. Paola Donfrancesco, in: Francesco Donfrancesco (ed.), *I fili dell'anima*, Bergamo (Moretti & Vitali) 2003, pp. 181-196.
2004g	"Il World Wide Web dal punto di vista della vita logica

dell'anima", (newly) transl. Luciano Perez, in: *Babele* 28 (Repubblica di San Marino) (December 2004), pp. 12-24.

D. Japanese

1987i   "Kodomo no kyûjo, ariuwa jikan no ôryo—Imi heno toi nitsuite" (= "Die Rettung des Kindes oder die Entwendung der Zeit", Japanese), transl. Toshio Kawai, in: *Shisô 759 (*1987), pp. 30-55.

1999b   "Danzetsu. Moshikuwa shinrigaku to shûkyo", in: *Asu e no Teigen: Kyoto Zen Shinpo Ronshu* [Proposals for Tomorrow: Selected Essays from the Kyoto Zen Symposium], Kyoto (Tenryûji Kokusai sôgô kenshûjo) 1999, pp. 55-73.

2000a   "Shinrigaku no mirai—sono botsuraku" (= "The Future of Psychology: Its Going Under", Japanese), in: Special issue on "New Perspectives in Psychotherapy in the 21st Century" of *Seishin Ryoho* [Japanese Journal of Psychotherapy], vol. 26, no. 1 (February 2000), pp. 33-40.

2003a   ("What Are the Factors That Heal?", Japanese), transl. Toshio Kawai, in: *Human Mind* No. 109, May 2003, Tokyo, pp. 114-125.

E. Portugese

1999f   "Matanças: O platonismo da psicologia e o elo perdido com a realidade", in: http://www.rubedo.psc.br/Artigos/mantancas.html.

2000f   "Uma Vez Mais a Questão Realidade/Irrealidade" (= "Once More the Reality/Irreality Issue", Portugese), transl. Simone Mesquita Rigueira, in: http://www.rubedo.psc.br/artigosb/realirea.html.

2003d   "O Terrorismo Islâmico" (= "Islamic Terrorism", Portugese), in: Luigi Zoja and Donald Williams (eds.), *Manhã de setembro. O pesadelo global do terrorismo*, São Paulo (Axis Mundi) 2003, pp. 65-85.

2005h   "Uma Conversa com Wolfgang Giegerich", in: *Cadernos Junguianos* 1 (2005), pp. 59-67.

2005i   "A difusão da WEB segundo o punto de vista da vida lógica da alma", in: http://www.ijrs.org.br/arigos.php?id=13.

2008h	[Open letter] "Carta Aos participantes do Seminário sobre James Hillman e Wolfgang Giegerich no Brasil", transl. Marcus Quintaes, http://www.himma.psc.br/artigos/artigo_12_2k8.htm.
2011c	"O pensamento de Jung acerca do Self à luz da sua Experiência Subjacente", transl. Alexandre Schmitt, in: http://grupohimma.blogspot.com/2011/02/o-pensamento-de-jung-acerca-do-self-luz.html.
2012k	"Um tributo a James Hillman" (= "A Tribute to James Hillman", Portugese), transl. Letícia Capriotti and Gustavo Barcellos, in: *Cadernos Junguianos* 8 (2012), pp. 89-108.

F. Czech

2001d	"Duše a internet (World wide web z pohledu hlubinné psychologie)", transl. Petr Patočka, in: *revue PROSTOR 52* (2001), pp. 75-90.
2002b	"Prefabrikovaný čas" (= "The Fabrication of Time", Czech), transl. Milan Jára, in: *revue PROSTOR 54* (2002), pp. 81-88.
2006e	"Islámský terorismus" (= "Islamic Terrorism", Czech), in: *revue PROSTOR* 69/70 (2006), pp. 189-205.
2007g	"Chvála zapomínání aneb 'Vzpomínková kultura' jako duševní fundamentalismus", in: *revue PROSTOR* 75 (2007), pp. 107-116.
2009e	"Ještě jednou k Ervinu Laszlovi a stavitelům mostů", in: *revue PROSTOR* 83 (2009), pp. 171-176.
2010f	Contribution to a discussion about a the question raised by Gerry Goddard "Může se současná astrologie stát mostem k novému integrálnímu světovému názoru, k vícerozměrnému obrazu člověka a kosmu?" (= W. G., "Idle Ideologizing", Czech), transl. Petr Lisý, in: *revue PROSTOR* 85 (2010), pp. 50-52.

G. Latvian

1991?	(Summary by) Roberts Mūks (Avens), "Vai tehnoloğijai ir dvēsele?", in: ??, pp. 127-134. 1991 ?
1991?	(Summary by) Roberts Mūks (Avens), "Kristiānisms un technoloğija", in: ??, pp. 22-27 and 34-39. 1991 ?
1992	(Summary by) Roberts Mūks (Avens), "Dievu metamorfoze.

Kristietība un tehnoloğija jaunā skatījumā: Volfgangs Gīgerihs" (= "Metamorphosis of the Gods. Christianity and Technology from a New Perspective: Wolfgang Giegerich"), in: *Grāmata* 1992 VII, pp. 3-95.

H. Spanish

2007a "Una lucecita que llevar a través de la noche y la tormenta. Comentarios sobre la situación actual de la psicología junguiana", in: http://homepage.mac.com/eeskenazi/gieger1.html.

2007b "Entrevista a Wolfgang Giegerich por Marcus Quintaes. Traducción del inglés por Enrique Eskenazi," in: http://homepage.mac.com/eeskenazi/quintaes2.html.

2007f "El significado de nuestro predicamento nuclear para la psicología analítica & de la psicología analítica para nuestro predicamento nuclear", transl. Enrique Eskenazi, in: http://homepage.mac.com/eeskenazi/gieger2.html.

2007h "El Presente como Dimensión del Alma El 'Conflicto Actual' y la Psicología Arquetipal", in: http://homepage.mac.com/eeskenazi/giegerpresen.html.

2007i "Matanzas. El platonismo de la psicología y el eslabón perdido con la realidad", transl. Enrique Eskenazi, in: http://homepage.mac.com/eeskenazi/gieger_kill.html.

2007j "Una vez más la cuestión de la realidad/irrealidad. Una respuesta a la respuesta de Hillman", transl. Enrique Eskenazi, in: http://homepage.mac.com/eeskenazi/giger_reply.html.

2007k "El error básico de la psicología de la oposición entre 'individual' y 'colectivo': reflexiones sobre el Magnum Opus de hoy del Alma", transl. Enrique Eskenazi, in: http://homepage.mac.com/eeskenazi/gieger_ind.html.

2008a "Epílogo de Wolfgang Giegerich a *Dialectics & Analytical Psychology: The El Capitan Canyon Seminar*", transl. Enrique Eskenazi, in: http://homepage.mac.com/eeskenazi/gieg_epi.html.

2008b "Prefacio a 'La Vida Lógica del Alma. Hacia uno Noción Rigurosa de la Psicologia'", transl. Enrique Eskenazi, in: http://homepage.mac.com/eeskenazi/gieger9.html.

2008c	"¡Sin coartada! Comentario a 'La Psique Autónoma. Una Comunicación a Goodheart desde el Campo Bi-Personal de Paul Kugler y James Hillman'", transl. Enrique Eskenazi, in: http://homepage.mac.com/eeskenazi/gieg_coartada.html.
2008f	"¿Es 'profunda' el alma? Introduciéndose y siguiendo el movimiento lógico del 'Fragmento 45' de Heráclito", transl. Enrique Eskenazi, in: http://homepage.mac.com/eeskenazi/gieger_logos.html.
2008i	"Carta de Wolfgang Giegerich a los participantes del *Seminário sobre James Hillman e Wolfgang Giegerich* en Brasil" [= "Letter from Wolfgang Giegerich to the participants at the James Hillman and Wolfgang Giegerich Seminar in Brazil"], transl. Enrique Eskenazi, in: http://homepage.mac.com/eeskenazi/gieg_carta2008.html.
2008j	"El Objeto de la psichología", transl. Enrique Eskenazi, in: http://homepage.mac.com/eeskenazi/gieg_objeto.html.
2008k	"La Historicidad del Mito", transl. Enrique Eskenazi, http://homepage.mac.com/eeskenazi/gieger_mito.html.
2008l	"La Huida al Inconsciente. Un análisis psicológico del proyecto de psicología de C. G. Jung", transl. Enrique Eskenazi, http://homepage.mac.com/eeskenazi/gieger_huida.html.
2009a	"W. Giegerich: Psicología y Verdad", summarized and transl. by Enrique Eskenazi http://homepage.mac.com/eeskenazi/gieger_verdad.html. "W. Giegerich: Psicología y Verdad (2)" http://homepage.mac.com/eeskenazi/gieger_verdad2.html.
2009b	"El Fin del Significado y el Nacimiento del Hombre: Un Ensayo acerca el Estadio Alcanzado en la Historia de la Conciencia y un Análisis del Proyecto Psicológico de C. G. Jung", transl. Alejandro Bica, rev. Enrique Eskenazi, (Part I) http://homepage.mac.com/eeskenazi/gieg_finsig.html and (segunda parte) http://homepage.mac.com/eeskenazi/gieg_finsig2.html.
2009g	"¿Esfuerzo? ¡Sí, Esfuerzo!" Fragmento del artículo en Spring 1988, en respuesta al artículo de James Hillman: "Hegel, Giegerich y los U.S.A.", transl. Enrique Eskenazi, in: http://tinyurl.com/yke57qp.
2009h	"Reflexión 'externa', reflexion inmanente y entendimiento", transl. Enrique Eskenazi, in: http://tinyurl.com/yea244f.

2010a	"La Falacia Ego Psicológica: Una Nota sobre 'el nacimiento del significado a partir del símbolo'", transl. Alejandro Bica, rev. Enrique Eskenazi, in: http://homepage.mac.com/eeskenazi/gieg_falacia.html.
2010c	"El psicólogo como predicador del arrepentimiento y evangelizador", transl. Alejandro Bica, rev. Enrique Eskenazi, in: http://homepage.mac.com/eeskenazi/gieg_repentance.html or http://tinyurl.com/yjm6ry9.
2010e	"'¡Prohibida la Entrada!' La Entrada en la Psicología y el Estilo del Discurso Psicológico. El 'quién' del discurso psicológico", transl. Alejandro Bica, in: http://homepage.mac.com/eeskenazi/gieger_quien.html.
2010g	"El gato que non es un gato", transl. Alejandro Bica, in: http://homepage.mac.com/eeskenazi/Gieger_gato.html.
2010i	"'Irrelevantificación' o: acerca de la muerte de la naturaleza, la construcción del 'arquetipo' y el nacimiento del hombre", transl. Enrique Eskenazi, in: http://homepage.mac.com/eeskenazi/gieg_irre.html.
2011b	"Primero la Sombra, luego el Anima, o el advenimiento del Huésped. La integración de la Sombra y el surgimiento de la Psicología", transl. Josep M. Moreno, in: http://homepage.mac.com/eeskenazi/gieg_sombra_anima.html.
2011d	"¿La realidad del Mal? Un análisis del argumento de Jung", transl. Enrique Eskenazi and Alejandro Bica, in: http://alebica.blogspot.com/2011/08/la-realidad-del-mal.html.
2011e	"Amar las preguntas mismas", transl. Alejandro Bica, in: http://alebica.blogspot.com/2011/11/amar-las-preguntas-mismas.html.
2012b	"La World Wide Web desde el punto de vista de la vida lógica del alma", transl. Helena Hinarejos Domènech and Alejandro Bica, in: http://alebica.blogspot.com/2012/01/la-web-desde-el-punto-de-vista-del-alma.html.
2012c	"Hillman y la vida sigue: los pensamientos de Giegerich", transl. Alejandro Bica, in: http://alebica.blogspot.com/2012/01/james-hillman-y-la-vida-sigue.html.
2012d	"El cierre y la liberación del espíritu embotellado de la alquimia y de la psicología", transl. Alejandro Bica, in: http://alebica.blogspot.com/2012/03/cierre-y-liberacion.html.

2012f	"El sacrificio de Isaac y la línea divisoria de la historia", transl. Alejandro Bica, in: http://alebica.blogspot.com.es/2012/05/el-sacrificio-de-isaac.html.
2012i	"La función de la televisión y el problema del alma", transl. Luis R. Álvarez, rev. Helena Hinarejos Domènech and Alejandro Bica in: http://alebica.blogspot.com.es/2012/09/la-television-y-el-alma.html.
2012j	"Acteón y Artemisa: La representación pictórica de la noción y la interpretación (psico-) lógica del mito", transl. Enrique Eskenazi and Alejandro Bica, in: http://alebica.blogspot.com.es/2012/09/acteon-y-artemisa.html.
2013b	"Alma y mundo", transl. Luis R. Álvarez and Alejandro Bica, in: http://alebica.blogspot.com.es/2013/03/alma-y-mundo.html.
2013c	"¡Dios no debe morir! La tesis de C. G. Jung sobre la unilateralidad del cristianismo", transl. Alejandro Bica, in: http://alebica.blogspot.com.es/2013/03/dios-no-debe-morir.html.
2013g	"'Conflicto/resolución', 'oposición/unión creativa' versus dialéctica, y el ascenso a la montaña resbaladiza", transl. Alejandro Bica, in: http://alebica.blogspot.com.es/2013/05/conflicto-resolucion-vs-dialectica.html.
2016a	"Psicología como anti-filosofía: C. G. Jung", transl. Alejandro Bica, in: http://alebica.blogspot.com.es/2016/01/psicologia-como-anti-filosofia-cg-jung.html.
2016d	"Dos Jungs. A propósito del artículo de Mark Saban", transl. Alejandro Bica, in: http://alebica.blogspot.de/2016/07/dos-jungs.html.
2016e	"Liber Novus, es decir, La Nueva Biblia. Un primer análisis del Libro Rojo de C. G. Jung", transl. Luis R. Álvarez and Alejandro Bica, in: http://alebica.blogspot.de/2016/10/analisis-del-libro-rojo.html.
2016f	"La procedencia de los hallazgos psicológicos de C. G. Jung", transl. Roberto A. Urrea Muñoz and Alejandro Bica, in: http://www.universoarke.com/revista-aion/numero-1-octubre-de-2016/la-procedencia-de-los-hallazgos-psicologicos-de-c-g-jung.
2017c	"Psychologie Larmoyante: Glen Slater, por ejemplo. Sobre el fracaso de la psicología para afrontar el mundo moderno",

	transl. Joan Martínez, Alejandro Chavarria, and Alejandro Bica, in: http://alebica.blogspot.com.es/2017/05/psychologie-larmoyante.html.
2018e	"Un serio malentendido: sincronicidad y la generación de significado", transl. Daniel Nellstrum Brown and Alejandro Bica, in: http://alebica.blogspot.com/2018/12/sincronicidad.html.
2019a	"La psicología junguiana: Una empresa sin base. Reflexiones sobre nuestra identidad como junguianos", transl. Joan Martínez, rev. Alejandro Bica, in: http://alebica.blogspot.com/2019/01/psicologia-junguiana.html.

I. Russian

1992h	"Выход из потока событий: Океан и кровообращение" (= Deliverance from the Stream of Events: Okeanos and the Circulation of the Blood", Russian), transl. А. Драгомощеико, in: *Митин журнал*, no. 43, 1992, pp. 108-114. Now: http://www.vavilon.ru/metatext/mj43/gigerich.html.
1992i	"Производство времени" (= "The Fabrication of Time", Russian), transl. А. Секацкого, in: *Митин журнал*, no. 47-48, 1992. Now: http://kolonna.mitin.com/archive/mj4748/giger.shtml.
1996f	"Ракета и стартовая площадка" (= "The Rocket and the Launching Base", Russian), transl. А. Секацкого, in: *Митин журнал*, no. 53, 1996, pp. 228-243. Now: http://www.vavilon.ru/metatext/mj53/gigerich.html.

J. Polish

2019b	"Psychologia jungowska—bezpodstawne przedsięwzięcie. Refleksje nad naszą jungowską tożsamością" (= "Jungian Psychology: A Baseless Enterprise. Reflections on Our Identity as Jungians", Polish), transl. Malgorzata Kalinowska, in: *RAVEN. Psychologie głębi u kultura*, 1(2019), pp. 7-17.

Index

A

abandonment 32
absolute 29, 81, 83–84, 87–88, 88, 111
  authority 37
  receptivity 29
  truth 22, 30
abstraction 43 (n. 1), 54, 55, 57, 73, 86, 108
Actaion 27–28, 30
Adams, Michael Vannoy 4, 28
alchemical opus 6
Alchemical Studies (Jung) 73
alchemy 6, 68, 73, 78
Alkmene 28, 35–36, 38, 40
Amphytrion 35–38, 40
analysis xv, 103–105
analytical psychology: *See* psychology: analytical
Anaximander 55
anima xiv, 88, 108–109, 111
anima-psychology xv: *See also* psychology: anima-only
animal rationale xix
animus xiv, 108–109, 109, 111
Animus-Psychologie (Giegerich) xiv
animus-psychology xv
anthropological constant 43
antinomies 83–84
Apollo 32, 93
archetype(s) 27, 43 (n 2), 64, 67
archetypes-in-themselves 43
Archimedean viewpoint 70

Aristotle xix, xx–xxi, 78, 81, 91
Athene 32
Aufhebung xv (n. 30)
Aus der Erfahrung des Denkens (Heidegger) xviii
axiom of internal relations 71, 74 (n. 25)

B

Bacchantes, The (Euripides) 96
Bacchus 95–97
Bachofen, Johann Jakob 26
Baudelaire 59
begetter 29–31, 33, 38
Berkeley, George (Bishop) xv
beyond 11, 12, 16, 22, 23, 36–37
Bion, Wilfred R. 65
Bluebeard 110

C

Camus, Albert 22
causality 67, 70
certainty 90, 93, 98
  self-identical 91
Coleridge, Samuel Taylor 86
collective unconscious 88
compensation 88, 92–93
complexio xiii, xiv
conception 29, 31, 33, 34
conflict 1, 2, 8
coniunctio 105, 112
conscious xiv, 92

consciousness xiv (n. 28), 5–6, 9, 12, 19, 42, 44–51, 53–57, 55, 71, 73, 78, 83 (n. 15), 85 (n. 19), 88, 90–95, 98–99, 101–102, 106, 110
  cultural xvii
  higher 82 (n. 11)
  implicit 53
  logical form of 99
  mythological-ritualistic stage/status of: *See* mythological-ritualistic stage of consciousness
  objective 53
  reasonable 51, 54
  subjective 53
contradiction(s) x, 2–3, 5–6, 8, 66–67, 74 (n. 25), 75, 77, 81–84, 90–91, 95, 97–98, 103, 105
  internal 61
corruption
  external 102
  fermenting 6, 32, 34, 100 (n. 61)
  internal 94, 102
  transforming 89
creative synthesis 5, 7
culture 51, 79, 88
cynicism 23

D

daimon xv
Danae 28, 33–35, 38, 40
depth psychology: *See* psychology: depth
Descartes, René 57
dialectic xiii, 2, 3, 8, 17, 22, 24, 26, 79, 81, 84, 85 (n. 19), 86–87, 90, 93–94, 98
  internal, of the position 16
  living 96
  self-contradictory 14–15

dialectic of interpretation 66, 79
dialectical change 7 (n. 8)
dialectical interiorization 11
dialectical model, Hester Solomon's 4, 6–7
dialectical movement 5–6, 8, 21, 62, 73, 77, 80, 85 (n. 19), 88, 99 (n. 59)
dialectical procedure 8
dialectical process 5, 6
dialectical thinking viii, xvii, xx, 2–4, 8, 61, 82 (n. 12)
  misconstrual of 3
dialectical unfolding 88–90
dialectics xix–xxi, 1–2, 4–5, 8, 25, 61, 82–83, 87, 90
Dionysos 31–34, 39–40
dismemberment 32, 34, 97
  initiatory 96–97
  of Pentheus 95–96
dream(s) xx (n. 56), 3, 8–10, 22, 41, 46, 52, 63, 78, 85–86, 88–89, 95–96, 102–103, 106
dream-ego 9, 95–96
dream-time 44–47, 49, 52–53
duality 39

E

ectopsychic functions xix
ego xii–xiii, xvi, 9–10, 18, 23, 85, 89, 92–93: *See also* ego-consciousness; ego-ideal; ego-instinct; non-ego; pleasure ego; reality ego
  negation of xv
  patriarchal 96
ego personality xv, 18
ego-consciousness xii–xiii
ego-difference xvi
ego-oriented view of psyche xiv

ego-perspective xiii
"ego-Self" axis xiii
ego-syntonic view of self xii
enantiodromia 91
Enlightenment 82
Erasmus 48
eros xiv, xviii
Euripides 96
extensio 110
exteriority 106
externality 21, 109
  negation of 16

F

fairy tale(s) viii, 10–13, 18–22, 44, 55 (n. 7), 73, 98, 103
faith 37, 50, 59, 65
fantasy 4, 19, 63, 65, 101–103
fantasy-image 65, 73, 80, 103
father 31, 34, 37, 38–39, 57, 102
feminine 28–29, 31, 96
Findlay, J. N. 101–102, 105
Fliess, Wilhelm 101
freedom 3, 84, 84–85, 85 (n. 21), 99 (n. 59)
Freud 101, 102, 103
Freud, Anna 91
Freud, Sigmund xii, xx (n. 56), 86, 89, 101–105

G

Gedankenschreck xx (n. 56)
Gehrts, Heino 49
Gelassenheit xviii
glass mountain 10–12, 19–23, 27, 36–37, 55 (n. 7), 73, 109
God 38, 57–58, 92
  death of 94
  dying 93–94, 94
god(s) 10, 28, 31–32, 35–37, 39, 57, 69, 95–97
golden apple(s) 11, 13, 19, 20, 27, 36
Gorgon 34
guilt 10, 56
  pure 56

H

Hades 110
Hebe 39
Hegel, G. W. F. xii, 4–9, 15, 51–52, 54, 57, 62–64, 71, 74 (n. 25), 75, 77, 81–86, 82 (n. 12), 88, 90, 94, 96–97, 99 (n. 59), 112
Hegelian dialectics xviii, 4, 7–8
Heidegger, Martin xviii–xx
Hera 35–39
Herakles 39 (n. 4), 39-40
Hercules 34
Hermes 31
Hesiod 45–46, 55
hieròs gámos 35–39
Hillman, James x–xi, xiii–xvi, 4, 15 (n. 11), 89, 94 (n. 46), 105–106
Hinterwelt 43
Holy Ghost 34, 38
Homer 45–46, 55
Hoppe, H. 4
Hume, David 67
hysteria 101

I

identification with the aggressor 91
identity 81, 84, 86, 91
  objective 54
  self-identical 87
identity of identity and difference 88: See also identity of identity and non-identity
identity of identity and non-identity

81 (n. 9), 83: *See also* identity of identity and difference
identity with the world 51–56
image
  inness in 49
  logical status of 49
image(s) xiv–xv, 37, 41, 46–49, 57, 77, 99–100, 109–112
  mythic 47–48
  reality of 49
  suggestive power of 47, 52
imaginal xiii–xiv, 8, 49, 55 (n. 7), 57, 67, 98, 109–110, 112
imaginal geography 111
imaginal psychology: *See* psychology: imaginal
imagination xv, 106, 109–112
imitatio Christi xi
immediacy 48–49, 54–55, 57, 74, 85 (n. 19), 110
impregnation 33–34
individuation 92–93
infantile sexuality 102
initial position 6, 84, 90, 94: *See also* Position
initiation 19, 34, 37, 39, 53, 56
inner infinity 86, 88, 103, 105
intellect xx, 50
intentio obliqua 3
intentio recta 3
interiority 9, 16–17, 21, 26, 71, 74–75, 85 (n. 19), 87, 109, 111
interiorization 15, 17, 18, 21, 23, 71, 99, 106
  absolute-negative 19, 24, 27, 98, 100, 103, 106
  negative 17, 20, 100 (n. 61)
interpretive principle
  Jung's 65, 68, 73, 80

J

judgment(s)
  a posteriori 67
  a priori 67, 68
  analytic 25, 61, 65, 66, 67, 70, 71
  analytic *a posteriori* 68, 74 (n. 25)
  analytic *a priori* 67, 68, 70, 71, 72
  self-referential analytic 68
  synthetic 25, 26, 30, 61, 65, 66, 67, 68, 70, 71, 90
  synthetic *a posteriori* 67, 68, 70, 72
  synthetic *a priori* 67, 68, 70, 78
Jung, C. G. xv–xvi, 7–8, 27, 29, 32, 41, 43, 52–53, 62–65, 67–69, 73, 75, 77, 80, 85–90, 92–93, 98–99, 104

K

Kant, Immanuel 25, 62, 64–65, 67–72, 74 (n. 25), 75, 77–78, 81–84, 90
Kant's Copernican revolution 67, 81, 83–84
Keats, John 93–95, 100
Kena Upanishad 27
Kerényi, Karl 32, 35, 42
Kierkegaard, Søren 65
knowledge 55, 59
  essential 53
  practical 53
Kore 34, 35, 110, 112

L

lapis 80: *See also* philosopher's stone
Law of Contradiction 81 (n. 10): *See also* Law of Non-contradiction
Law of Identity 81 (n. 10)
Law of Non-contradiction 81 (n. 10)
Le bourgeois gentilhomme (Molière)

INDEX

41
Lévi-Strauss, Claude 51
Lévy-Bruhl, Lucien 51–52
locus
   of knowledge 42, 44, 53, 54, 56
   of man's spiritual life 50
   of myth 50
logic xvi–xviii, xx, 6, 26, 31, 52, 68, 70, 81 (n. 11), 84
   formal xix, 82 (n. 12)
   internal 29, 42
   objective 54
   self-defining 74 (n. 25)
   traditional 82, 82 (n. 12), 84
logical life viii, xviii, 2–3, 3, 108
   self-contradictory 84, 85
logical motion 21, 26
logos xiv, xviii, 26, 52, 54, 56–58, 96

M

maenads 96–97
marriage 1, 35, 37–39
masculine 28–29, 31
matter xiv–xv, 79–80, 83, 86, 109: See also prima materia; prime matter
mea culpa position 93 (n. 42)
meaning
   religious 37
Medusa 34
mercurial soul 111
mercurial spirit 2 (n. 1), 15 (n. 11), 109
mercurial success 18
Mercurius 105
metaphysical man 54, 58
metaphysics xix, 40, 55, 58, 83 (n. 15)
   age of 58
   medieval 57

Western 57
methemerinoì gámoi 35
Midgard Serpent 45
mind 3, 5, 8, 16, 21–22, 29, 32, 34, 37–38, 43 (n. 1), 51–59, 62, 67, 69, 70, 78, 82–84, 86, 92, 100 (n. 61), 101, 110–112
   metaphysical 58 (n. 8)
   natural 58
   objective 51, 52
Mnemosyne 93
mode of being-in-the-world 43 (n. 1), 54, 57, 59: See also mythic mode of being-in-the-world; mythological-ritualistic mode of being-in-the-world; religious mode of being-in-the-world; ritualistic mode of being-in-the-world
modernity 58–59
Molière 41
mortificatio 89
mother 31–34
motherhood of Zeus 31
mountain: See glass mountain; slippery mountain
Mueller, G. E. 4
Murphy's Law 90
myth
   living 45
Myth of Sisyphus (Camus) 22
myth(s) 26, 29, 30, 32, 41–44, 46, 49, 51–52, 55–57, 59, 64, 96–97
   Actaion-Artemis 26–28
   Alkmene 30, 36, 37
   as narrative 42
   as nature's knowing 50
   living 42
   Semele 30, 34
   Sisyphus 10, 18, 22

study of 29
sun 69
mythic mode of being-in-the-world 43 (n. 1), 45–46, 48–49, 56
mythic thinking 43 (n. 1)
mythic-imaginal conception of the world 55
mythological man 58
mythological-ritualistic mode of being-in-the-world 40, 42, 49
mythological-ritualistic stage of consciousness 44, 51, 55 (n. 7)
mythos 52, 54, 58

N

narrative form 13, 43 (n. 1)
narrative(s) 8, 13–14, 18, 20, 26, 42–45, 49–50, 55
nature 32, 37, 49–50, 53, 56, 58
  sublation of 32
negation xx, 8, 12, 14–17, 20, 22–24, 56, 67, 81–82, 88, 91–92, 101, 105–106, 109–110
  absolute 6, 12–13, 103
  logical 93
  recursive process of 6
  second-order 94
  simple/first 90, 92–95, 98
negation of the negation xx, 6, 12, 14–16, 18, 20, 22, 24, 89, 90, 92–95, 97, 100
negation of the initial position 6, 16
negative xvii, 97
negativity 15, 18, 19, 24, 75, 91, 106
  absolute 8–9, 11, 18–21, 27, 98–101, 106
  reflective 91
neurosis 1, 102
Nicholas of Cusa 57
Nietzsche, Friedrich 73–75, 89, 94

non-ego 18
non-identity 81–83
numinosity 100
numinous 56, 99, 100

O

object xiv (n. 28), 26–27, 37, 48, 72, 74, 83 (n. 15), 86
  external 105
  image as, of consciousness 110
  transitional: *See* transitional object
object relations 2, 26
object(s)
  significant 50
objective mind 51, 52
objective psyche 52
Objective Subject 21
objectivity 50, 68
Oedipus complex 102
Olympus 39
Opening up of the Access to Myth, The (Kerényi) 42
opposites 4, 5, 7, 8, 95
  bipolar 5
  tension of 7
  union of 5–6, 31
opposition 81 (n. 9), 83 (n. 15)
  external 109
other 26, 31, 33, 36 (n. 3), 36–37, 63, 72–73, 84–86, 88–90, 92, 99, 102, 110–111
  external 17, 63, 86, 109, 111
  internal 26, 29, 63, 71–72, 74, 85–86, 89, 110–111
  literal 26
  Zeus as 38
otherness 36, 38, 99, 109

P

paradis artificiels 59

INDEX

participation mystique 51
pathologizing 89
peace negotiation 4–5
peak(s) 108, 109: *See also* peak(s) and vale(s)
and vale(s) 15 (n. 11), 109, 111–112
Pegasus 34
penetration 30
Pentheus 95–97
Persephone 34, 112
Perseus 34, 40
philosopher's stone 80–81, 106
philosophy 40, 57, 62–65, 71, 75, 82
 Hegelian 8, 63–64, 81
 Kantian 69, 81, 83 (n. 15), 84
 medieval 51
 of Antiquity 57
Pinkard, Terry 4
Plotinus xx–xxi
Position xvii, 5–6, 8, 12, 16, 20, 71, 84, 90–92: *See also* initial position
position(s)
 psychological 108
 self-identical 85
positive reality 16, 19, 24, 37, 49
positivity 13–14, 16, 17–20, 22–23, 39, 48–49, 75, 100, 102–103, 105
pregnancy 39
prelogical mentality 51
prima materia 78, 81, 83: *See also* prime matter
prime matter 6, 78–81, 84, 86, 89, 99, 105: *See also* prima materia
Proclus 35
projection xii–xiv, 63
Pseudo-Democritus 58 (n. 8)
psyche viii–x, xii–xiv, xvi, 3, 43, 52, 69, 70, 78, 84, 89, 96, 99–100
 archaic 11
 ego-oriented view of xiv
 non-egoic hegemony of xv
 polythestic xiii
 positively existing 43
psychoanalysis 78–79, 89, 101, 103–105
psychological difference 2, 12, 52, 102
psychological man 50, 58
psychological phenomenology 43
psychological transformation xvii, xviii
psychological typology 41–42
psychology viii–ix, ix, xii, xvi, xx–xxi, 26, 28–29, 62, 69–70, 74–75, 81, 96, 102–104, 108–109
 analytical 4, 69
 anima-only 112
 archetypal x
 depth ix, xii, xiii, 69, 86
 ego 112
 humanistic xii
 imaginal 109, 110, 112
 personalistic xii, 112
 polytheistic xiv
 pop ix
 radical xx
 true 77, 101, 103–106
psychology project 62, 63, 75, 102
psychotherapy 104
punishment 10, 56

Q

quaternio 36, 36 (n. 3), 38–39

R

Radin, Paul 51

reality 5, 13, 19, 29, 35–36, 39, 47–48, 50, 52, 55, 71, 82 (n. 12), 83, 111
  archetypal 26
  empirical 17, 22
  external 26
  image 49
  literal 24
  objective, of causality 67
  ordinary 19, 20, 22
  positive 43, 48
  pragmatic 35
  sensual-imaginal 56
  social 36, 39
  subsisting 50
reality principle 9
recursive progression 15
referent 48–49, 105
religion(s) 23, 37, 40, 57, 58, 79
religious mode of being-in-the-world 39, 57
resignation 23
resistance 95
resolution 2
Restored Position 13, 20, 21
ritual(s) 44, 45, 50–52, 54, 57
ritualistic mode of being-in-the-world 51

S

scepticism 23
Schopenhauer, Arthur 58
seduction theory 101–102, 105
Self xiii, xv, 92–93
self xii–xiii, xv, xx–xxi, 86, 92, 99, 109
self-abandonment 29, 30, 31, 33
  absolute 34
self-application 17, 109
self-closure 45
self-consciousness 57, 59, 86, 91
self-contradiction 3, 15, 16, 21, 23, 74 (n. 25), 81, 83–89
self-development 29
self-duplication 86
self-evidence 52
self-expression 42
self-identity 84, 85, 87, 88, 89, 91
self-movement 110
self-negation 16
self-realization xi, 22
self-relation 26, 30, 72, 74, 99
self-revelation 63
self-sacrifice xi
self-sameness 91
semantics 43, 57, 93, 110, 112
Semele 28–33, 35, 38, 40
semen 33–34
sensual-imaginal 54–56
shadow 63
shame 95, 95 (n. 47)
signatura rerum 51
Sisyphus 10, 15, 18, 22
slippery mountain 9, 11, 14, 24, 27, 28
Solomon, Hester 4–7
soul xiii–xvi, xx–xxi, 2, 8, 9, 12, 16, 18–19, 23–24, 26–30, 32–39, 43–44, 49–50, 58, 70, 75, 78, 85 (n. 19), 87, 89, 96, 98, 103, 106, 108–112
  analytic unfolding of 30
  land of the 21, 22, 24, 27
Soul's Logical Life, The (Giegerich) viii, xiv, xviii, xx, 4, 26, 28, 92
space
  intensional 16
  logically negative 16
  negation of 16
spirit xiv–xv, 34–35, 57, 78, 82

INDEX

(n. 11), 86, 88, 96–97, 106, 108–109, 111: *See also* mercurial spirit
subject xiv (n. 28), 2 (n. 1), 20–22, 26–27, 33, 43, 46, 67, 72, 74 (n. 25), 78, 86, 97, 105: *See also* Objective Subject; subjective subject
   analytic 74 (n. 25)
subject-object split xiv (n. 28)
subjective subject 21–22
subjectivity 50, 57
sublation xv (n. 30), 32, 94, 95
suggestion 103, 105
symbol 26, 32, 99
symptom(s) 88–90, 109
syntax 43, 57, 93, 95, 102, 110, 112
syzygy xiv, 96, 111

T

Teleía 35, 37
teleology 44
Tertullian 29
Theogony (Hesiod) 45
theology 93
thesis—antithesis—synthesis 3–4
thing-in-itself 23, 83 (n. 15)
thinking xviii–xix, xxi
   calculative xviii
   deconstructive 9
   implicit xix
   meditative xviii
   positivistic 7
thought xiv (n. 28), xv, xix–xxi, 5, 8–9, 18–19, 21, 24, 45, 57, 64, 67, 70–71, 83, 87, 90, 98, 100 (n. 61), 101–103, 106, 108–111
   flight from xx
   Hegelian 7, 62
   implicitness of 99

Jungian vii, x, xv, 64
   metaphysical 58
   philosophical xii
   primary laws of 81 (n. 10)
   speculative 105
   unconscious xx
Thus Spoke Zarathustra (Nietzsche) 89
Thyone 30
total vision 98–100
transcendence 12–13, 16–19, 21–24
transcendent function 7
transference(s) 87–89
transitional object 79
truth 17, 20, 26–30, 47–50, 53–54, 56, 58–59, 68, 81, 83, 88–90, 96–97, 100 (n. 61)
   absolute 28
   archetypal 27
   communal 48
   event of 27
   inner 18
   moment(s) of 26–28, 36–39
   mythic 46
   naked 26–28, 30, 36
   notional 19
   ocean of 47, 53
   psychological viii
   religious 48
   self-sufficient 54
   ultimate 30
   virginal 30

U

unconscious xii–xiv, 1, 7, 16, 23–24, 37, 43 (n. 2), 63, 69, 85 (n. 19), 88, 92, 98
underworld 33–34, 39, 39 (n. 4)
union 30, 32–34, 37, 39, 40, 42
   Alkmene's, with Zeus 40

balanced 35
between gods 35
creative 61
of opposites 5–6, 31
of the soul with itself 32–33, 35
sexual 35, 38
unity 81 (n. 9), 83, 97
   inner 72
   of myth 42
   of narrative and mythic status of consciousness 43 (n. 1), 46
   of psyche and logos 96
   of semantics and syntax 43, 43 (n. 1)
   of the intellectual and the natural 51
   syzygial 111
   transcendent 87
   with nature 56
unity of identity and difference 85–86, 88, 90, 94, 96–97, 103, 105: *See also* identity of identity and difference; unity of the unity and difference
unity of the unity and difference 3, 84, 111: *See also* identity of identity and difference; unity of identity and difference

V

vale(s) 108, 109, 111: *See also* peak(s) and vale(s)
Virgin Mary xiii, 34, 38
volition 49: *See also* will

W

will xii, 3, 25, 46, 56, 84, 85 (n. 21)
willing 3, 25, 84, 85
wine 32
Winnicott, D.W. 78–80
womb 31–34
Wordsworth, William 100
World as Will and Idea, The (Schopenhauer) 58
world tree 55 (n. 7)

Z

Zeus 29–40
   Teleios 36

Milton Keynes UK
Ingram Content Group UK Ltd.
UKHW010444080224
437402UK00021B/253